THE BEST of SCOTTISH POETRY

An Anthology of Contemporary
Scottish Verse

Edited by
Robin Bell

Chambers

The publisher acknowledges subsidy from the Scottish Arts Council towards the publication of this volume.

British Library Cataloguing in Publication Data

The Best of Scottish poetry: an anthology of
    contemporary Scottish verse.
    1. Poetry in English. Scottish writers, 1945–
    Anthologies
    I. Bell, Robin, 1945–
    821'.914'0809411
ISBN 0–550—21014–8

Jacket design by James Hutcheson
Typeset by Buccleuch Printers Ltd, Hawick
Printed in Great Britain at the University Press, Cambridge

INTRODUCTION

This book aims to find out what living Scottish poets think·about
their own poetry. I wanted to draw together the best writing by
Scots poets from all over the world and also record the sort of
personal insights that sometimes happen in conversation but are
rarely set down on paper.

I would never claim that this book contains 100 per cent of the
best living Scottish poetry but I believe you will find, like the best
whisky, it has a very healthy percentage proof.

How did I go about collecting these poems? I wrote to the Scots
whom I consider to have written the best poetry or song lyrics and
asked the bluntest of questions: 'If you were to be run over by a bus
tomorrow, which three pages of your poetry would you most like
to be remembered by – and why?'

I made it clear that I was not looking for a definitive judgement,
just an insight into how these writers see their work so far. I did not
pretend it was an easy question nor that writers are necessarily the
best judges of their own work, but I wanted a book that
unashamedly backed the individual and gave him or her the room to
succeed. Norman MacCaig replied, 'Dear Robin, you've asked me
to do a thing I hate doing – write about me and, even more, about
my verses.' He did it anyway. I'm grateful to him and all the others.
There was a generosity of spirit that made the anthology fun to edit.

Each poet receives the same amount of space, except for the
Gaelic poets where translations have also been included. The poets
are arranged by surname, rather than by age, because I do not want
to create the impression that a living sixty-year-old poet is
automatically less 'modern' than a living thirty-year-old. In any
case, alphabetical order makes for more amusing bedfellows and
more surprises than strict chronological order.

The poets went about their selections in their own ways. William
Montgomerie managed the almost impossible task of reflecting
most of the main aspects of a long career within three pages. Robert
Allan Jamieson, thinking about his transition from writing in
English to Shetlandic, said, 'Looking at these poems as some sort of
origination and destination, I see the journey more clearly than I
might have done if I had considered every turning step along the
way.' Kathleen Jamie chose to include her most recent poem and
was not at all sure about wanting to preserve her work if she were

struck down by my mythical bus: 'All books should be burned, say, 80 years after the author's death. We have no problem with the mortality and regeneration of cabbages and kings, shoe-laces and electric kettles, so why should books be preserved?' Liz Lochhead disarmingly said, 'Why did I choose these poems? Because, I suppose, I must like them the best.'

The one thing that came across consistently, despite all the different backgrounds and perspectives, was the poets' passionate commitment to poetry. To keep on writing good poetry requires discipline and hard training, just like a professional sportsman, with the same possibilities of success and failure. Like the best players, the best poets entertain by knowing just when to be serious about their work and when to make fun of it.

Writing poetry may be a private activity, but printing it is as public a form of communication as writing a newspaper feature or a TV news story. Poetry can belong anywhere, not just in a literary context. For example, Alastair Fowler's powerful poem, 'Exodus', about childbirth and mortality, appeared in the medical journal, *Developmental Medicine and Child Neurology*. Alastair Reid summed up very well the sense of purpose and shared experience in poetry: 'I look on poems much as I look on recipes: they do not do the cooking for you, but they help.'

I have tried to present the poems and writers' comments in the same way as they arrived individually at my house. As you open them, I hope you share some of the curiosity and expectation that I had. I cannot imagine ever becoming so blasé that I lack a flicker of excitement when the postman hands me a large green tube sent from 'Little Sparta' and I wonder what Ian Hamilton Finlay has put inside it and can the printer do it justice?

In 1945, the year I was born, Maurice Linday edited an excellent book, *An Anthology of the Scottish Renaissance*. It showed clearly how Hugh MacDiarmid and his contemporaries had produced sparkling poetry as a reaction to post-Victorian stodge. William Soutar, however, who wrote in a robust Perthshire dialect, had a poem which began, 'Noo that the Scots Renaissance's owre and dune'. He wrote that as long ago as 1932, yet even today many Scots fondly imagine this old renaissance is enough to provide inspiration for younger poets writing at the end of this century. If you look at anthologies since 1945, you would think that Scottish poetry had had more renaissances than a phoenix on a trampoline, each with slightly less fire and bounce than the last. It's not an accurate picture.

Forget about renaissances. They end up as mannerism, where style is more important than content and everything is packaged up into designed themes. The strength of today's Scottish poetry is in its diversity. This book includes poetry not just in the various languages of Scotland itself but by Scots who, in a pattern familiar for centuries, have gone abroad and added to their own enterprise the best qualities of other cultures.

I sometimes wonder what would have happened if Roberts Burns in 1786 had gone off to the West Indies as he had planned? He had booked his passage to Kingston, but the woman with whom he was going to emigrate died and another woman at home bore him twins. If he had boarded the ship, would we now be hailing him as a great Jamaican poet? Given his 'Ode for General Washington's Birthday', would he have gone north to become the great poet that the American Revolution dearly wanted and never had? The serious point behind this speculation is that Scots remain Scots when they go abroad and that is why writers like Alastair Reid and Kenneth White bring another distinction to this anthology different from, say, the great Gaelic poems of Sorley MacLean.

The poems in this anthology are predominantly in English. That is the poets' choice. I'm glad we have strong Gaelic poetry and good work in regional Scots dialects. I'm not sorry that there is little Lallans. I regard it as a wasteful distraction for Scottish poetry that such a great poet and persuasive personality as Hugh MacDiarmid should have reached his peak at a time this century when there was a fashion for synthetic languages. Bernard Shaw was an advocate of Esperanto, but he had more sense than to write his plays in it. Lallans, begotten of Jamieson's dictionary with its tabular juxtapositions of words from different centuries and regions, was always too artificial to be an effective means of communicating with the general reader. What matters is not the size of a poet's Scottish vocabulary but its integrity. Having said that, I would always argue strongly for the writer's right to express himself in any form he wishes, so long as he accepts that the reader has equal rights.

You will find here work by people whom we would think of as songwriters, rather than as poets, because Scotland has such a powerful ballad tradition and because words out loud are no less valid than words on the page, I am glad to include writers like

Ewan MacColl and Midge Ure. I am also glad to have the shapely work of Ian Hamilton Finlay. I was lucky enough to have a positive response from nearly everyone I wanted to have in the book and I am grateful to them and to their publishers.

It is customary in an introduction to give a snappy round-up of trends in contemporary poetry. However, since forty-two good brains have gone to the trouble of making their own comments on their poems, I will attempt no further analysis. In any case, I was put off literary criticism long ago by Douglas Young, a fine Scots poet and elegant Greek scholar. I had read the term 'Caledonian antisyzegy' which appeared to have some profound significance for Scottish poetry. I had got as far as working out that it meant some form of contradiction or paradox, when I asked Douglas Young what an antisyzegy was. 'It is the sound MacDiarmid makes when he sneezes,' Young replied.

I did my best to select the best living Scottish poets, without any artificial checks or balances. Looking through them now, they turn out to be a multifarious lot: Highland, Lowland, immigrant, emigrant, Protestant, Catholic, Jew, atheist, young, old, male, female, rich ones, poor ones, big fat ones, little thin ones, urban, rural, serious ones, funny ones, immaculate ones with tasteful ties, scruffy ones, solid placid ones, terrible fidgets, bred from the best girls' private schools and from tough comprehensives, loud ones, quiet ones, with a range of politics and sexual proclivities as various as the work itself. But you don't need me to tell you that. Look at the poems.

Robin Bell

CONTENTS

ROBIN BELL

Born in Dundee in 1945 and grew up in Strathearn. Lived in New York and London, working in publishing and university teaching till he returned to Scotland in 1979. Five books of poetry published. Most recent is *Radio Poems* (Peterloo, 1989) which includes documentary poems broadcast by the BBC. Edited *The Collected Poems of the Marquis of Montrose* and other literary/historical books. He is secretary of the Poetry Association of Scotland.

'The Wooden Curlew' is about how inanimate objects and small creatures make their way in a world which we sometimes imagine to be controlled totally by humans. Of course you can't anthropomorphise everything or you'd keep ending up with Mrs Tiggiewinkle, but I find that metaphor helps me to express abstract concepts in a clearer, more tangible way.

'Sawing Logs' is about inheritance in its broadest sense. I dislike clichés about 'having to find yourself' and 'learning to like yourself' as if our personalities were objects that we could mislay or evaluate according to changing fashions in the Sunday papers. I never liked debates about whether our lives are genetically pre-programmed or alterable by learning new behaviour patterns, because it seems impossible to quantify in any useful sense. I believe there is more to be learned from the rituals of childhood and the interplay between the generations. I grew up in a rural manse. It is no coincidence that many writers of previous eras had the same background.

'Nancy Scott' is one of sixty characters from 'Strathinver', a portrait of a Scottish village from 1945–53. The radio version of 'Strathinver' won the Sony Award for the best British radio feature or documentary in 1985, the first time that poetry had won Britain's top broadcasting award. I had to devise a narrative form that was strict enough to tell an anecdote succinctly and pack in period detail, but flexible enough to let actors vary the pace and deliver punch lines. We had a lot of fun with it as a stage show.

THE WOODEN CURLEW

She was the extra decoy,
the one who looked different
to make the others credible.
She served her purpose
in the first hour of October light
amid the guns, the wounded splashing
and the black ripples
of the swimming dogs.

As daylight grew stronger
the gunfire tailed away.
Its sharp smoke slipped from
the hanging willow branches
while the men packed up their gear
into the green Range Rover
and drove off. She was left,
forgotten in the lee of a birch root.
She wintered there with weathering paint,
attracting real wildfowl to the safety
of the shallows by the empty hides.

The March floods lifted her
from her black nest in the withered reeds.
Slower and heavier with the winter's weight
of water in her frost-sprung grain,
she bobbed across the lake
and in the false dawn saw
the headlights cross the misty ridge
and park beside the water.
She saw the men launch the punt
and lay the mallard decoys
in a floating line.
There was no wooden curlew
to make them real. Still,
uncertain of what she had become,
she kept her distance from the slanting guns.

SAWING LOGS

My father, once in a while, would sit
beside the logpile as if to discover
how many days' warmth were left in it;
and I'd say, while he still thought it over,
'It's a good day for sawing, isn't it?'

The sapling rowans by the gate were bare
and the deer down early from the hills.
We needed more logs; I'd sit and pare
an apple with my penknife till
he said, 'You're right: there's not much there.'

The saw-horse stood in the back yard
with a stack of split planks, barrel staves,
lopped limbs from trees, old stakes and spars
from the garden: all the spare wood saved
since the first signs that winter would be hard.

We'd check for knots or awkward grain
and lay wood firm across the forks.
Setting the saw, my father would explain
how to go steady, make the blade do all the work.
I'd rush and buckle, have to start again.

The wood is scored to guide the blade;
the wrists bear down, the shoulders brace.
I'd saw from the forearms, but my father said,
'You'll tire yourself out. Saw from the waist
and put your whole back into it instead.'

Only well-seasoned wood is fit to burn;
anything green will wait a few weeks yet.
Once our stroke ran smooth, the stack was turned
into long-houred logs. He'd take a hatchet
and split some kindling when we'd done.

The saw did our speaking. The sharp air
drew out our breath. The wind was cold;
but we were warm and making warmth out there.
He was near seventy. I was twelve years old
and four hands on a saw was all we were.

NANCY SCOTT

Respectable folk said Nancy Scott was 'loose',
seeming to overlook the obvious fact
that the bits of her that showed were much too tight.
Her clinging red sweater never quite
restrained her good points. Her belt was wide and black,
patent leather like her high-heeled shoes.

She was the star of local teenage dreams
and figured in middle-aged nightmares too,
for Nancy had a smile that seemed to show
just how well she knew you by her 'Hello'.
Peter Jones the draper denied he knew
where she got nylons with such perfect seams.

She didn't mind what the busy gossips said,
even enjoyed it, because it let her
make fun of prudes. She tried to be seen to flirt
with them, or greet couples, straightening her skirt,
with, 'I hope your back is feeling better',
and watch her face go white and his go red.

ALAN BOLD

Alan Bold was born in 1943 in Edinburgh, writes regularly for the *Glasgow Herald* and is the author of many volumes of verse, including a selection in *Penguin Modern Poets 15* and *In This Corner: Selected Poems 1963–83*. He is well known as a critic for his books on *Modern Scottish Literature*, *The Ballad*, *Muriel Spark* and *MacDiarmid: A Critical Biography*.

I have chosen three contrasting poems for specific qualities I regard as vital to the creation of verse, since I believe, with Ezra Pound, that technique is the test of sincerity and that the poet must offer more than self-indulgent free-association. Poetic language becomes an acceptably human reality only when it reaches outwards to communicate instead of forever retreating inwards to comfort. Artistic insight should, I feel, be informed by intellect and controlled by craft.

'One Woman' is an exploration of the territory each individual regards as inviolable. It imposes a psychological strain on a given scenario, pressurising iambic rhythms and formal stanzaic patterns to renew the tradition of the dream-poem in a contemporary situation. Through close observation of an actual figure in a particular landscape, it confronts the central character as a stranger in a familiar environment. Eventually, however, the poem reaches a conclusion that reveals the woman's social perception of herself.

'A Special Theory of Relativity' reflects my interest in the imaginative challenge of imagery with its universal implications. Thematically, it relates one of the key insights of the century to the subjective experience of sexual love. Structurally, it expands on a resonant refrain, advancing by varying the theme. It is a love poem with a speculative point.

'Notice on MacParnassus' is a somewhat mischievous quatrain, playing a little conceptual game with the duality of the Scottish poet who has meant most to me and whose biography I spent several years writing.

ONE WOMAN

One woman walks beside a running stream,
The rush of water agitating her.
She stares at thrusting bushes, feels the tips
Of rhododendron leaves, regards the pink
Blossoms as her own. They brush her hips
As she comes closer to the riverside.
Blue flowers seed around her, she conceives
Another human being could be near.
She pats her stomach, lies down on the bank.
She shuts her eyelids. She begins to dream.

Inside her head, the semblance of a stage
Assembles. The actors rehearse their roles,
Squabbling over which parts they should read.
A leading lady, features like her own,
Floats about her business, unconcerned
As scores of suitors try to pin her down.
At last, the great surrender: on the bed
She moans her triumph, totters on the edge
Of madness, shudders as he sheds his seed.
She knows her lover could be anyone.

The solstice moon is sliced in two: the bright
Half, basking in reflected glory, glows
In startling contrast to the unlit half
Which looks transparent on the blue beyond.
Life conceived in contrasts: day and night,
Light and dark, good and evil, near and far.
Illusions are reality, a grand
Delusion that locates a swelling star
Within the reach of hand, the grasp of mind.
The sun defeats her purpose as it grows.

Soon, clinging by the roots of her sweet place,
She tests the temper of the weather. Wind
Whips up a hurricane of hatred, rain

Nourishes the bark and branches send
Leafy messages to surrounding skies
With no pathetic fallacy in sight.
A tree, being without a human brain,
Endures the everyday assault, its space
Insulted by its toxic injuries
And, branches saturated, slowly dies.

Her eyes are open, she perceives the world
As part of an untidy cosmic plot.
Herself a gardener, in the old wives tales,
She parts the grass, reveals the earth beneath.
She starts to dig. She makes a shallow pit,
Tossing the stones into the running stream.
The sun dissolves into the dark, the dream
Dissolves into the dirt. She feels the bones
Of some long-buried woman like herself
And goes on scratching with her fingernails.

A SPECIAL THEORY OF RELATIVITY

According to Einstein
There's no still centre of the universe:
Everything is moving
Relative to something else.
My love, I move myself towards you,
Measure my motion
In relation to yours.

According to Einstein
The mass of a moving body
Exceeds its mass
When standing still.
My love, in moving
Through you
I feel my mass increase.

According to Einstein
The length of a moving body
Diminishes
As speed increases.
My love, after accelerating
Inside you
I spectacularly shrink.

According to Einstein
Time slows down
As we approach
The speed of light.
My love, as we approach
The speed of light
Time is standing still.

NOTICE ON MACPARNASSUS

The hill was high, I really wouldnae hairm it
    Yet had to leave.
It said: 'Reserved for Hugh MacDiarmid
    (Signed) C M Grieve.'

GEORGE MACKAY BROWN

I was born in Stromness and only left there to attend Newbattle Abbey College and Edinburgh University. After lean early years, I can now live by writing – not, alas, by poetry, which is the greatest kind of literature. But I try to let the poetic imagination into my stories and novels, not by the back door, but as an honoured guest.

'Hamnavoe' is an elegy for my father, a postman. I try to imagine Stromness (Hamnavoe) as it might have seemed to him in the early 1900s. Another Orkney place that has kindled my imagination is the sea valley of Rackwick in Hoy. It has been a place teeming with the children of crofter-fishermen. Until recently it seemed threatened with complete depopulation. Now many of the ruins are being restored.

The poem 'A Child's Calendar' tries to see this beautiful place, throughout one year, with 'the innocent eye'. It is next to impossible to suggest the full range of one's poetry in three poems. Lest any cynical reader think I am only capable of the slackness of free verse – which, believe me, is the most difficult kind to handle, since it calls for a highly developed sense of rhythm and of essential form and of the deeper music of words – I include 'Taxman', which rhymes throughout and has a steady beat. I try to get the essence of country life and work in Orkney into as few words as possible. They had to work hard for any festivals they celebrated: Harvest Home, the Lammas Fair, Yule, Johnsmas. Over all fell the shadow of the laird and his factor. The dues had to be met. Such a brief poem couldn't include other hazards: tempest, the worm in the corn, the long summer droughts.

HAMNAVOE

My father passed with his penny letters
Through closes opening and shutting like legends
    When barbarous with gulls
    Hamnavoe's morning broke

On the salt and tar steps. Herring boats,
Puffing red sails, the tillers
    Of cold horizons, leaned
    Down the gull-gaunt tide

And threw dark nets on sudden silver harvests.
A stallion at the sweet fountain
    Dredged water, and touched
    Fire from steel-kissed cobbles.

Hard on noon four bearded merchants
Past the pipe-spitting pier-head strolled,
    Holy with greed, chanting
    Their slow grave jargon.

A tinker keened like a tartan gull
At cuithe-hung doors. A crofter lass
    Trudged through the lavish dung
    In a dream of cornstalks and milk.

In 'The Artic Whaler' three blue elbows fell,
Regular as waves, from beards spumy with porter,
    Till the amber day ebbed out
    To its black dregs.

The boats drove furrows homeward, like ploughmen
In blizzards of gulls. Gaelic fisher girls
    Flashed knife and dirge
    Over drifts of herring,

And boys with penny wands lured gleams
From the tangled veins of the flood. Houses went blind
    Up one steep close, for a
    Grief by the shrouded nets.

The kirk, in a gale of psalms, went heaving through
A tumult of roofs, freighted for heaven. And lovers
    Unblessed by steeples, lay under
    The buttered bannock of the moon.

He quenched his lantern, leaving the last door.
Because of his gay poverty that kept
    My seapink innocence
    From the worm and black wind;

And because, under equality's sun,
All things wear now to a common soiling,
    In the fire of images
    Gladly I put my hand
    To save that day for him.

A CHILD'S CALENDAR

No visitors in January.
A snowman smokes a cold pipe in the yard.

They stand about like ancient women,
The February hills.
They have seen many a coming and going, the hills.

In March, Moorfea is littered
With knock-kneed lambs.

Daffodils at the door in April,
Three shawled Marys.
A lark splurges in galilees of sky.

And in May
A russet stallion shoulders the hill apart.
The mares tremble.

The June bee
Bumps in the pane with a heavy bag of plunder.

Strangers swarm in July
With cameras, binoculars, bird books.

He thumped the crag in August,
A blind blue whale.

September crofts get wrecked in blond surges.
They struggle, the harvesters.
They drag loaf and ale-kirn into winter.

In October the fishmonger
Argues, pleads, threatens at the shore.

Nothing in November
But tinkers at the door, keening, with cans.

Some December midnight
Christ, lord, lie warm in our byre.
Here are stars, an ox, poverty enough.

TAXMAN

Seven scythes leaned at the wall.
Beard upon golden beard
The last barley load
Swayed through the yard.
The girls uncorked the ale.
Fiddle and feet moved together.
Then between stubble and heather
A horseman rode.

GEORGE BRUCE

George Bruce was born in 1909 and brought up in Fraserburgh, where the family had lived at least since the eighteenth century. His main collections are *The Collected Poems of George Bruce* (1970) and *Perspectives* (1987). In 1982 he was appointed Scottish/Australian Writing Fellow.

'Inheritance' was written in the early 1940s. It lifted me out of the confusion and despair created by imprisonment in a purposeless, indifferent society, cut off from its past, and by the war. A whole people survived 'the sea obstinate against the land'. Their lives were not impoverished.

Forty-three years after 'Inheritance' the sea remains the ultimate measure in 'Old Man and Sea' but now is a time for reflection in the presence of its beauty and terror. The old man makes his way through a less intransigent landscape – there are rambler roses, though it is less secure – the iron gate trembles. He is alone in the presence of a mystery, or is he alone? Is the presence by which he must find his being in him? There is a hint of an inheritance.

'Rembrandt in Age', a self-portrait in the National Gallery of Scotland, shows the darkness and also the intense life of the eyes – 'the window to the soul'. But 'soul' in English is too abstract, so I prefer the more intimate, more physical Scots, which is nearer to Dutch than English.

'Laotian Peasant Shot' – the most successful short poem I ever wrote – is a rejoicing in mere being. The 'exultation' is in the perfect balance of natural man. There follows the momentary awareness of the impending extinction of identity. The theme is sustained through the poem by images of life – 'air', 'wind', 'breath', in association with images of death. (There is one word for all three in Hebrew: the poem is in the form of a psalm.) This event I saw on a small screen, which reduced the difficulty of sustaining that poise essential to the imaginative artist of detachment and engagement.

In 'Tower on Cliff Top, Easter 1968', a poem for my wife, the intense experience of love projects itself 'in sudden glare and roaring airs'. We are part of this enlivening nature. It is the day too of the resurrection, when a broken day was made whole.

INHERITANCE

This which I write now
Was written years ago
Before my birth
In the features of my father.

It was stamped
In the rock formations
West of my hometown.
Not I write,

But, perhaps William Bruce,
Cooper.
Perhaps here his hand
Well articled in his trade.

Then though my words
Hit out
An ebullition from
City or flower,

There not my faith,
These the paint
Smeared upon
The inarticulate,

The salt crusted sea-boot,
The red-eyed mackerel,
The plate shining with herring,
And many men,

Seamen and craftsmen and curers,
And behind them
The protest of hundreds of years,
The sea obstinate against the land.

OLD MAN AND SEA

Nightfall – was it still out there?

The rusty, white iron gate trembled
as it opened to the path to the sea
down by the ramblers, unseen,
no scent, for the salt had taken over.
With all my fearing childhood in it
I hear it growling in the dark. Ahead
from where the marram grass meets sand,
between me and the slapping water – a figure:
he stands square-shouldered staring
into that nothing.
          How many mornings
when the silvered horizon promised,
giving hope for that day
or when the mist stood impenetrable,
or when the sky burst and the sea met it,
I thought, he waited, thought I knew him,
might approach, touch him, claim him for kin,
he who stood his ground for us all,
but there is no reckoning in this matter.
Square-shouldered I stood looking into that nothing.

REMBRANDT IN AGE

He kent, as thae een lookt at his
oot o the dark he made in yon picter,
he lookt on a man, himsel, as on
a stane dish, or leaf faa'in in winter,
that calm was his strang seuch.
But in the dark twa wee lichts,
een that shone like lit windaes,
an in that hoose muckle business,
words an kindnesses atween folk.
Aa that steir in Rembrandt's heid,
or, as some wud say, in's verra saul.

LAOTIAN PEASANT SHOT

He ran in the living air,
exultation in his heels.

A gust of wind will erect
a twisting tower of dried leaves
that will collapse when
the breath is withdrawn.

He turned momentarily,
his eyes looking into his fear,
seeking himself.

When he fell the dust
hung in the air
like an empty container
of him.

TOWER ON CLIFF TOP, *Easter, 1968*

When I took your hand, securing
you at the turn of the stone stair,
for the narrow step deepened by unknown
steps that climbed that dark,
(many generations in that dark
that split the day from day)
the sky broke blue above;
below the stone cube, the flat sea,
then in this place we knew
what we had known before
the years grew in us together,
yet never knew as here and now
in sudden glare and roaring airs,
as time had waited on this time
to know this in our broken day
when I took your hand.

RON BUTLIN

Ron Butlin (born 1949, Edinburgh). He has been a computer operator, security guard, footman and model, as well as Writer in Residence at the University of Edinburgh. He has published three collections of poetry, a book of short stories and a novel. His work has been broadcast and translated both in Europe and North America.

'Inheritance'. This poem speaks in what I recognise to be my 'authentic' voice: the same voice that narrated my first short story (the title of which was given to the collection – *The Tilting Room*): the same voice that is central to my first novel *The Sound of my Voice*. In this poem, arising from one of my earliest memories, the 'adult-me' – as it were – talks to the 'child-me' through his first experience of guilt and, thereby, through his childhood *Fall* into Time. Simply, it is the poem that comes closest to my understanding of things.

'Portrait of a Shadow-sailor'. I never use simile but the form of extended metaphor in this poem allowed me to explore what previously I had only *sensed*, and very dimly at that. The shadow-sailor's voyage is mine and yet, so I've been told, seems like enough to certain other people's experience as to give the suggestion of not travelling alone. When I was younger I rejoiced in a suitably romantic isolation; the reception of this poem has given me a more enriching perspective: the celebration of what men have in common.

'Mozart'. Music is very important to me but for a long time, Mozart was a puzzler. I could not see what all the fuss was about – his tunes seemed to burble along happily like a kind of eighteenth-century muzak. Then, at last – I *heard* him. Suddenly everything changed and from that moment the world has never been quite the same. This short poem is the earliest of the three, and the slightest, but records one of my most joyful discoveries.

INHERITANCE

Although there are nettles here, and thorns,
you will not be stung. Trust me, I've something
to show you made from twigs, bird-spittle, down
and journeyings in all weathers.
See how easily your hand covers
the nest and its eggs. How weightless they are.
Your fingernail, so very much smaller than mine,
can trace the delicate shell's blue veins
until they crack apart, letting silence
spill into your hand. There is a sense
of separation almost too great to bear
– and suddenly you long to crush all colour
from these pale blue eggs, for in their brief
fragility you recognise as grief
the overwhelming tenderness you feel.
This is your inheritance:
your fist clenched on yolk and broken shell,
on fragments of an unfamiliar tense.

PORTRAIT OF A SHADOW-SAILOR

At thirty-five years old
he's halfway round his lifetime's only world
– quite at sea. (*That* at least, is true).
By day he plays the captain and the crew
Whose rank and medals have been tattooed on
– gentle pinpricks cutting to the bone.
At night he lies and listens: the crow's nest sways
almost audibly above, and weighs
out silence for the darkened scene below
– letting the slightest measure only, flow
into his sea-crazed mind.

Tightening his grip upon the helm
(in 'lock-position') the shadow-sailor calms

approaching storms by will-power. He reshapes
the cliffs and waves according to his maps;
their tears and creases mean what *he* decides
in terms of shallows, hidden reefs. He prides
himself upon a life's experience
of reading charts long out of date: he glides
across the wind-scarred surface, making sense
of every ocean-contour (this one hides
a bogeyman within its childish scrawls,
and that one traps a god). Such reverence!
In these deserted sea-lanes he collides
with ghost-ships – their slow and soundless passage falls
shadowless across his decks and hull.

   Sea-wraiths and the demons who preside
upon the ocean-floor advise him; coral
(saturated with the sudden cries
of drowning men) signifies their power.
These are his familiars; their histories
are his; their voices he alone can hear;
their silence is the elemental measure
of despair.
          Thus his world has taken shape:
a place of terror, clashing rocks, the hiss
of cross-run currents, undertows to rip
his soul apart . . .

   His log's kept neat for he believes that this
– i.e. the mastery of words, and clear
calligraphy – improves the truth. His fear,
therefore, must complement the sentence-structure
or be dropped. Each entry's much the same;
new page, top left: 'The heat, the chill, the heaving
sea beneath are everything I know . . .'
Yet sometimes he can sense a tide whose flow
runs greater, and carries to a farther shore:
Too briefly, then, he'll glimpse and recognise
what lies beyond this shadow-sea, these shadow skies.

As evening falls he watches ocean-colours
and the sun dissolve into each other,
letting their transparency reveal
the night sky and the ocean-floor:

The heavens' slow creation and destruction
the shadow-sailor takes into himself,
letting constellations drift at random:

– until he's made, of stars and minerals,
the darkness his imagination spills
unearthly light upon.

MOZART

He is very clear water
that seems only a few inches deep,
and yet you will never, never
touch the bottom

or, you will walk upon the surface
thinking that this is easy
and not in the least miraculous.

STEWART CONN

Stewart Conn was born in Glasgow and now lives in Edinburgh. His latest volume *In the Kibble Palace* is published by Bloodaxe. Recent work as a dramatist includes the screenplay for *Blood Hunt* (BBC2) and two stage plays, *By the Pool* and *Hugh Miller*, both premiered during the 1988 Edinburgh Festival.

'Under the Ice', the title-poem for one of my collections, is simply a personal favourite. Its central images are from a letter of Coleridge's, and a portrait in the National Gallery. It ends up (like others I've written) a love-poem, without my having had this consciously in mind, at the outset.

'Springtime' reflects, I suppose, that sense of the precarious which permeates my poetry. Its presence on the closing page of my *New & Selected Poems* suggests a significance to me in what it tries to express, no matter how simple that may be, or how persistently it has been said previously.

One always hopes new work will be detectably different from what has gone before, while retaining an individual imprint. 'Renoir in Orkney' (the most recent of these three) is one of a group on the painter and his painting. It stemmed from a stay in Stromness, followed shortly after by a visit to Les Collettes, in the south of France, where Renoir spent his last years.

UNDER THE ICE

Like Coleridge, I waltz
on ice. And watch my shadow
on the water below. Knowing that
if the ice were not there
I'd drown. Half willing it.

In my cord jacket
and neat cravat, I keep
returning to the one spot.
How long, to cut
a perfect circle out?

Something in me
rejects the notion.
The arc is never complete.
My figures-of-eight
almost, not quite, meet.

Was Raeburn's skating parson
a man of God, poised
impeccably on the brink;
or his bland stare
no more than a decorous front?

If I could keep my cool
like that. Gazing straight ahead,
not at my feet. Giving
no sign of knowing
how deep the water, how thin the ice.

Behind that, the other
question: whether the real you
pirouettes in space,
or beckons from under the ice
for me to come through.

SPRINGTIME

In front of me a girl with bare feet,
in a beribboned dress, picks white
flowers in a field somewhere near Pompeii.

Each day I look at her, head straight,
right hand outstretched as she delicately
plucks the stem. Was she there that night

the lava flowed, birds shrivelled in the sky
and lovers turned to ash, where they lay?
If so, what had she done to deserve it?

I wonder, will it ever be
Springtime again, the blood flow freely;
or has man blighted all hope of recovery?

We are on borrowed time, you and I,
and have been from the outset.
All that is left, is to live lovingly.

RENOIR IN ORKNEY

Monet might have made himself at home
among these flat, green islands
like giant waterlilies. Cezanne even,
with cliff-faces all cones and cylinders.

Not that my vision is impaired.
More a narrowing of the spectrum
to a harmony of glistening silk,
as though too much light were being let in –

but without the embracing warmth
to which I am accustomed: seascape
and skyscape, a constant radiance.
It would need the skin of the place

to burst a blood vessel, or myself
to stab at it with my palette knife:
then there'd be something I could express.
Only this morning, the world disappeared;

the boat I was in surrounded
by quicksilver; the bordering land
erased in mist. Like a composer
frantic for some variation

beyond a single high-pitched note
sustained in his brain,
I crave a cacophony of colour,
before my mind disintegrates.

At least with the fishermen
I am at home. Their tanned features
merit the mixing of pigments:
my yellows and reds are in business again.

As for the womenfolk, baiting the line
has made their fingers like my own,
and worse: knife-gashes, to the bone.
Nudes are out. For one thing, their Kirk

concedes no such tradition.
For another, contemplate the climate.
But something in me burns. I must
start again. I have found a girl

with skin like mother-of-pearl;
am working on still lives of lobsters;
and will distribute at the solstice
canvases of wild flowers, like mottled flame.

DOUGLAS DUNN

Douglas Dunn was born in Renfrewshire in 1942. His most recent books are *Elegies* (1985), *Selected Poems* (1986) and *Northlight* (1988), all published by Faber & Faber. He lives in Tayport, Fife.

'The Apple Tree' considers a standard, negative assessment of Scotland and Scottishness, which the poem tries to dismiss. It also attempts a reconstructed spiritual identification with place, and a renewed love of it. My religious feelings are unorthodox and multiple, so terms like 'salvation', 'covenant', 'faith', 'missionary', and 'Gods', lean towards paganism instead of replicating a presbyterian vocabulary. That the terms overlap is, I hope, provocative, suggesting that the one exists in the other. Few things delight me more than a Scottish orchard, first in the May-time, then in the days of its harvest. Also underlying the poem is a feeling that can be described in Heine's words: 'Do you hear the bell ringing? Kneel down – They are bringing the sacraments to a dying God.' If anything, the poem carries the indigenous and sacramental as a prayer against a large death.

I doubt if there's anything special about being a Scottish writer, but at least you can rhyme 'Bach' and 'loch'. Our rhotacistic 'r' also enables rhymes like 'moors/conifers', 'administered/transferred', and 'stars/disperse'. Rhymes exercise on metrical equipment in the gymnasium of the mouth, and the measure that I find encourages the noise I like in poems is iambic tetrameter. These, though, are fiddling, obsessive, technical points. 'Loch Music' pleased me when I finished it because while I was writing I felt that the poem challenged me with a feeling I couldn't articulate. It's set in Galloway. So, too, is 'The Apple Tree'.

The two poems are from *St Kilda's Parliament* (1981), published by Faber & Faber.

THE APPLE TREE

'And if the world should end tomorrow,
I still would plant my apple tree.'
Luther

I could play the bad eras like a concertina.
Multiple chords would squeak like 'Excuse me',
'I beg your pardon', 'Oops' and 'Sorry, no thank you.'
Pump hard on a squeeze-box and you can almost hear
The Protestant clerks of northern Europe in Hell,
Complaisant men who filled the paperwork of death
Or signed the warrants, exemplary in private life
But puritanical before their desks of duty.
Say what you like, their Gods did not approve of them.

Men moaned of Scotland that its barren air and soil
Couldn't so much as ripen an apple. I can hear
Their croaked whispers reproach the stern and wild of Alba,
Naming our Kirk, our character, our coarse consent
To drunken decency and sober violence,
Our paradox of ways. Here, in the lovely land,
Beside Kirkmaiden, enumerating apple trees,
I feel the simple millions groan, 'Keep you your faith.
A sapling nursed to fruit impersonates salvation.'

Tonight I saw the stars trapped underneath the water.
I signed the simple covenant we keep with love.
One hand held out an apple while the other held
Earth from a kirkyard where the dead remember me.
In these lost hollows of stern conventicles
A faith is kept with land and fruit. Already are
New scriptures written by the late-arriving autumn,
That postponed shuffle of leaves, that white frost-writing.
These are my missionary fruits, a kindred taste.

Then let my Gods be miracles brought on stone boats
By Conval and the first dailyday folk before him.
Rather an ordinary joy – a girl with a basket,
With apples under a linen cloth – than comfortless
With windlestrae to eat. Forge no false links of man
To land or creed, the true are good enough. Our lives
Crave codes of courtesy, ways of describing love,
And these, in a good-natured land, are ways to weep,
True comfort as you wipe your eyes and try to live.

LOCH MUSIC

I listen as recorded Bach
Restates the rhythms of a loch.
Through blends of dusk and dragonflies
A music settles on my eyes
Until I hear the living moors,
Sunk stones and shadowed conifers,
And what I hear is what I see,
A summer night's divinity.
And I am not administered
Tonight, but feel my life transferred
Beyond the realm of where I am
Into a personal extreme,
As on my wrist, my eager pulse
Counts out the blood of someone else.
Mist-moving trees proclaim a sense
Of sight without intelligence;
The intellects of water teach
A truth that's physical and rich.
I nourish nothing with the stars,
With minerals, as I disperse,
A scattering of quavered wash
As light against the wind as ash.

G F DUTTON

Anglo-Scots parentage, life mostly among Scotland's boulders and
scrub, urban or rural. One-time well-known scientist, climbing-
editor; honorary member of foreign universities, Scottish
Mountaineering Club and so on. Now drawing own conclusion,
partly in two books of verse, *Camp One* (Macdonald, 1978),
Squaring the Waves (Bloodaxe, 1984); both received Scottish Arts
Council awards.

These poems were chosen for diversity. Somebody might like
something. Also, diversity best illustrates whatever unity I seek.
Hopefully, what I do builds up and fills in. Now for what I *think* I
meant:

'salmon' was an (early) invocation for something to surface. Salmon
pools apparently inspired old Celtic verse; more importantly, there
is one beside my house. Like the bards, I need the touchable: 'no
ideas but in things'.

So the next two affirm the life behind the rocks and concrete of
Scotland; what we have made of them, they of us. My 'urban' verse,
especially, celebrates the bruised fist that shapes (or flinches from or
breaks) the technological flint; but 'ticket' merely records loss of
grasp, the amputation of a culture. The last two derive from years of
day-long wild-water swimming, which – like ventures into
mountaineering, landscaping, laboratory science – grapples more
personally with the physical Given. 'littoral' repeats that joy of
making, of construction (including destruction) among the flux:
your shaped flint, squared wall, planned experiment, bomb or poem
survives because it has *been*, is stamped beyond time. All my verse
explores such exploration, trying to portray compassionately how
human action – overt or implied – is fired by imagination beating
upon reason, barbarian upon Rome. This essential partnership is
emphasised in 'return', which reasserts a painfully reluctant (how
reluctant!) refusal to drown contentedly among (whatever) alluring
waves. Visions are shored by their reawakening. One is supported,
at the edge of the salmon pool, by cold wet stone against the knees.

SALMON

it has been a long silence.
perhaps one should approach
carefully the place, perhaps the fish
great silver fish
are tired and have gone back
nosing the cold stones
into the silver and black
behind the white waterfall.
for it is late and when we passed that tree
a leaf fell; and far, how far, downstream
summer and the sea.

hasten, for the wind may soon
unhook distraction, raining
thick, the water move and break,
the waterfall
become uncertain, blown
back to the rocks, unsteady.
hasten, part the quiet unmown
grasses carefully, and watch
the pool. for not again will fathoms burn
so lucidly for you, nor out of darkness
hugely to you the rising silver turn.

AS SO OFTEN IN SCOTLAND

as so often in Scotland
the sun travelled
dyke over dyke, burning
dead grass golden and ending,
after a wallow of foothills,
on one brown summit;
that flared its moment, too,
and was gone.

THE HIGH FLATS AT CRAIGSTON

the high flats at Craigston stand
rawboned in a raw land,
washed by thunderstorm and sun
and cloud shadows rolling on

from the bare hills behind, each one
out-staring the wind;
that every night
cling together and tremble with light.

TICKET

there has been
no summer and the road has ended
at a broken cliff. that hut

should have been the ferryman's
but he is out
and no one in

but an old woman talking to hens
and her son
has a good job in the town

will not be back
maybe the second week maybe
december, that was his car

I did not see
on this bare island with one road,
cliffs at both ends.

LITTORAL

waves beat in,
rocks withstand;
this white ocean
this grey land

play creation
in the round
of the sun's leisure.
and I swim here

take my pleasure
not in sea
not in shore
but one clean stroke

after another,
that wave and rock
pick up, throw back
between them for ever.

RETURN

I come from the sea.
there is salt on my lip.
I have lain on the sand
in the waves' retreat,
I have raised myself up
and trembled, been met
by battering light,
untouchable air;
and still stand here
bearing my weight,
trying to re-gather
trying to command
foot after foot
to climb the shore,
persuade my mind
to understand
why I must suffer
myself to land.

IAN HAMILTON FINLAY

Ian Hamilton Finlay began by writing short descriptive essays which were published in newspapers. Subsequently, with the addition of dialogue, these became short stories, and with more dialogue one-act plays for radio and television. In all these forms he was concerned with the idea of an ordered simplicity, and this reappeared in his concrete poetry as well as (later) in his gardening and landscaping. In addition to books, booklets and cards, he has published poster poems and poem-prints; his work is represented in art galleries and he has landscaped public garden-sites in America and Europe. It is difficult to say whether the First Battle of Little Sparta, at which Finlay and his associates confronted Strathclyde Region over the status of his garden temple, was a 'battle', an 'artwork' or an 'art event'. Biography, he has said, is inevitably inaccurate, and autobiography is not only inaccurate but unbecoming as well.

'Ring of waves' – this poem is unusual in concrete poetry in that it possesses a simple narrative. A fishing boat puts out to sea, fishes, and returns; the 'ring of light' at the end contrasts with the 'ring of waves' at the start of the poem; it is both the domestic lamplight (in the fisherman's home) and the idea of civilisation or culture, as opposed to nature (the waves). The opposition *nature/culture* often occurs in my work.

'Song/Wind/Wood' – three words are permutated, to give a concluding 'stanza' which – with the addition of the hyphen after 'wood' – reads 'woodwind song'. The words, inscribed in Roman letters on slate, are set in a small pine-grove, and the sound of the wind in the pine-boughs is intended as part of the work. Unassuming as the 'poem' is, it acknowledges a tradition of. pastoral, which reaches back to antiquity.

'Evening will come' – The 'blue sail' is perhaps the sky, in which case what is 'sown' are the stars, resembling stitches in a boat's sail. The effect is suggestive in the way that fragments sometimes are. I am enthusiastic about the Greek Presocratics – philosophers who came before Plato and whose work survives only in fragments or who wrote in fragment-like aphorisms like Heraclitus.

Some 'Detached Sentences' relating to the poems:

The Muse of concrete poetry reversed Mnemosyne's gift; depriving the poet of song, she gave him sweet eyesight.

Concrete poetry is less a visual than a *silent* poetry.

Concrete poems are sometimes thought childish because they are seen but not heard.

In the beginning was the word. And then there was syntax.

In conventional poetry adjectives are the heroes, in concrete poetry, nouns.

Language is part of us – but strange to us.

Environmental art, fully understood, means The Revolution.

From the author's *Table Talk*.

RING OF WAVES

ring of waves
row of nets
string of lights
row of fish
ring of nets
row of roofs
string of fish
ring of light

With Maxwell Allan. Photograph by Martyn Greenhalgh.

EVEN
-ING
WILL
COME

THEY
WILL
SEW
THE
BLUE
SAIL

ALASTAIR FOWLER

Alastair Fowler, born in Glasgow 1930, now divides his time between Edinburgh, where he was Regius Professor of Rhetoric and English Literature 1972–85, and the University of Virginia. He has edited *Paradise Lost*, and is the author of *Kinds of Literature* (1982) and *A History of English Literature* (1987).

My poems are sometimes called difficult, but (as I hope this selection shows) they are not so intentionally. I came to poetry late, so that being able to write poems is something I can never take for granted: when I found someone had memorised 'Edinburgh Sky Line' (Catacomb Suburb, 1976) it mattered to me. I like the way this poem gets in quite a few things (architectural and anatomical), and the way it stands up to oblivious banality my making the commercial sign overlap with the myth and excitement of the real city. 'Exodus' (from the same collection) draws on memories of attending my daughter's birth in 1954. It is characteristic in dealing with different areas of experience simultaneously: not only dying, but childbirth (it was reprinted in *Developmental Medicine and Child Neurology*).

John Ruskin's large social vision had impressed me long before I saw a carriage of his at Brantwood. I like 'Mr Ruskin Chooses a Travelling Carriage' (*From the Domain of Arnheim, 1982*) for communicating itself implicitly – through images of vehicles, for example: the well-prepared pleasure coach, the triumphal chariot, the early ambulance of the awesomely dedicated Baron Larrey. Poetry that will 'be' as well as 'say' is my aim, I suppose; and I have tried to realise Ruskin's coach through stolen Victorian phrases. Perhaps the poem catches something of tradition – our need to face the challenges of the past, our duty to a dedication we now fall short of.

EDINBURGH SKY LINE

City of stiff men: your skylines are not
Inhibited. Nibbling gorgeous Aurora,
The crow-stepping with dragon tips meets a cornice
Skirting in Flemish curves to jam fat rolls.
And even this oven warm baker's window
(What a moulding!) says MORNING ROLLS HERE.
I well believe it – wearing surely her wrap-
Around dress, but not too far. She leans
Over to serve the immediately half-awake,
Or sun diffracts through glass and lace, reflects
On glossy buns in crackling hot beds
Of percale paper. The sign calls for more
Than window-shopping: stand at the counter
Firmly: 'One morning please, tightly rolled.'

EXODUS

A long-watched-over much-bewildered labour,
And then, out of the body of my love, I saw
The red sea part and parcel of delivered life:
A miracle worked for. This prodigious change
Of form sustained, undergone, taken
By strenuous hope: this was the main thing:
Inaction left for grandiose smiles of fulfilment;
Not the tears and mess and blood below.
When my term comes, without sufficient practice
In arts of dying, may they yet reflect,
The always young midwives, while they shoulder
My stiffened legs, after retentive struggles,
How great release of life can come to be.
– Before they go about their brisk skills.

MR RUSKIN CHOOSES A TRAVELLING CARRIAGE

Mechanical requisites first: steady strength –
Poise of persons – easy rolling, and then
Stateliness to abash plebeian gazers.
The intricate high hopes! The complex joys
Of planning grand accommodations for triumphs!

Savour the cunning cellars under the seats,
Secret drawers below the anterior windows,
And highly invisible pockets, safe from dust.
– Half the comfort depends on a perfect fit
(Of fully-fashioned doors and windows too).

The pockets are easily accessible
To us by insidious slits, let in
Under the lining pads. They underlie
The padded lining. And the necromantic valves!
More delicate repose solicits rounding

Of each corner, smoothly. And best have
A small seat for father, in case of storms.
These plans of imagined trips cost no unease.
The singing intervals and passes of Europe
Open out.
            But it was not enough.

All we have dreamt of security is not
Enough. The courier still stationed behind
Continually whispers, and still the motto
Spells from the painted arms on the polished side:
Vix ea nostra voco. Next,

Or round the next corner, the hermetic sealer
Drives in his black trap; or others in hearses
Pulled by slow-moving plumed mares.
Less: a two-wheeled cart would do the thing,
Baron Larrey's dripping ambulance.

And yet uncounted turns of earth remain,
With many journeys. We need to spend a lot
On a vehicle of quite another colour,
Which will take us out to see the whole world
With a first stage burn fierce to consume our fears
And launch us as far as Ruskin might have strolled.

VALERIE GILLIES

Valerie Gillies was born in Canada in 1948, but grew up in Scotland. She attended the Universities of Edinburgh and Mysore, South India. Poet, freelance writer, collaborator with artists and musicians. Wife of William Gillies, Professor of Celtic: three children. Lives in Edinburgh. Currently Writer-in-residence at Duncan of Jordanstone College of Art.

I am the last person in the world to choose which poems to select from my work. I would rather leave that to readers of the future to decide. For me, the best things I've written are always the most recent. Let these three represent, then, a breakthrough in experimentation, let them show what the word can do, moved by music, rhythm and a thought. My work is about love, about landscape, it says Man *is* the landscape.

THE BROCKEN SPECTRE

On the May morning I flew to Orkney
I thought the loveliest thing in the sky today
Would be your head, my darling man,
Where it travels everywhere within mine.

When I overtook the wind and the birds in flight
I kept the thought of you with me as the very type
Of male beauty, your shapely skull and weatherbeaten skin,
While the plane bucked north into a strong headwind.

With my back to the sun and out of the blue
Supported within heaped cloud, I flew
Where I saw through the window, in mid-air reflection
Gliding and straying over cloud, a strange apparition.

Some metres off, the rising sun gave me the spectral sight
Of a circle displaying colours by refractive light:
At the nucleus of brilliant hues in a series of bands
Was the image of a head, emanation of an aerial man.

It floated alongside me, the whole spectrum in the ring.
I flew on: the spectre did the same.
Was something visible in the play of colour, or nothing but
The way in which light rays are broken up?

That it was my own thought, is the simple explanation,
Haunted by a handsome man in rainbow precipitation
Through air and water, mediating elements
Whose laws impress themselves upon my sense.

My illusory hope, to reach that airy sphere
From which you derive your features here:
When I looked for you and saw you in that light
You gave such radiance that angels couldn't be more bright.

Your painted head, full of chromatic possibilities,
Is where colours can discover themselves perfectly.
It's true, your form might go out into the spaces of the air
Across the gap between me and your spectre there.

What does the pilot think, used to seeing a halo above ground?
Or do I follow my delusion alone, my darling, in the round?
Like the small plane and its luminous target-mark
We think we are separate, but we are not.

TO A BUTTERFLY IN AN OVERGROWN GARDEN

This butterfly to the flowerhead clings,
forming a new and fairer flower of wings.

You give up your own identity:
now, are you flower or butterfly?

It's in the nature of the pretty
to survive by mimicry.

I look down on you from above:
who gave the self away for love?

You look up at me from below
and use your wings to go.

If I see you in terms of me,
refresh me with your ambiguity.

FRUID WATER

Fruid Water, furthest of all from the sea,
yours is the voice that means far more to me
than the salty wave flowing up the beach
of a great stretch of ocean I may never reach.
Little I care for foaming breakers on the shore
or the surface calm that moves so much slower
if I hear your notes that are sweeter than the surf
of all the different waters of the earth.

I don't need to see the whale or sea-wrack,
the flight of the gannet, the diving of the shag,
I long to watch your trout or your owl flying low,
on your banks I hear the sudden hooves of the roe.
Each of us finds that you can quench our thirst,
stream and surrounding terrain belong together from the first.
In the face of the light you become, through your quality,
like an eye reflecting us in transparency.

Huge masses of water roll in the oceans,
deep currents circulate, of gigantic proportions,
but where you flow freely and trickle over stones
you play with waves in rhythm, vibrate and sing alone.
Out of vapour you have come back to liquid,
you return in your course every time to Fruid.
Evaporating, loop with air currents and precipitate:
between earth and heaven you mediate.

Your moving form issuing from the hills
twists in strands of water changed like turning veils;
they make a rope that spirals down the glen,
new water falling through it to refresh men.
I can tell by the current as it swirls along
where it comes from, what rocks cause its tension,
and I praise your wave shapes through which the water flows,
for they remain the same, and rarely go.

DUNCAN GLEN

Duncan Glen was born in Cambuslang, Lanarkshire, in 1933. His
In Appearances, from which 'My Faither' and 'The Gullion' are
taken, was published in 1971. This has been followed by many other
books of poetry, including *Realities* (1980) from which the other
two poems come. W & R Chambers published his *Hugh
MacDiarmid and the Scottish Renaissance* in 1964. He edited *Akros*
poetry magazine from 1965 to 1983.

I choose these poems because I see each of them as a celebration of
the joy in life, not least 'My Faither' in which a man looks down at
his faither/father in his coffin. I chose two of them, but again
perhaps even 'My Faither', because they are poems of love – which
is the greatest celebration of life. Love is also a form of play and so is
all art, not least poetry rooted, of course, in a joy in the 'play' of
words even when at its most serious. And in this play, often, is
humour, and so I have chosen 'The Gullion' and 'Stranger in Toun'
because they end, at least for me, with humour. And so with our
common humanity.

I did not consciously decide to do so, but I have chosen poems
which build up from a lot of detail, of specifics. I see this as another
expression of the rich and diverse joy that is in life. My use of the
Scots language, particularly in 'My Faither' and 'The Gullion', is an
aspect of this diversity from the particular, although as I write the
words, for me they have several layers of meaning and reference.

As I have said, I wished my selection to reveal joy, but I also wanted
it to show an awareness that in our individual lives we always die a
little as life progresses – we lose as well as gain. Our 'faither'
becomes our 'father' as we move towards our own death which is,
of course, itself part of the cycle of renewal – of life. We lose the
'innocent' gullion of our childhood as we gain a new, and different,
awareness of it in later years. But I have chosen these poems because
I hope that within this more 'aware' stance remains something of
the 'innocence' that is part of the joy in life.

MY FAITHER

Staunin nou aside his braw bress-haunled coffin
I mind him fine aside the black shinin range
In his grey strippit troosers, galluses and nae collar
For the flannel shirt. My faither.

I ken him fine thae twenty or mair years ago
Wi his great bauchles and flet auld kep;
And in his pouch the spottit reid neepkin
For usin wi snuff. My faither.

And ben in the lobby abune the braw shoon and spats
Aside the silk waistcoat and claw-haimmer jaicket
Wi its muckle oxter pouch, hung the lum hat.
They caa'd him Jock the Lum. My faither.

And nou staunin wi thae braw shinin haunles
See him and me baith laid out in the best
Black suitin wi proper white aa weel chosen.
And dinna ken him. *My father.*

THE GULLION

I can mind the gullion
ayont the midden and the auld Alvis.

I can mind the ducks waddlin out the gate to dook.
And Peter goose takin out his wives
through the slap – hissin and streekin his neck.
The gullion for cuttin nettles wi a scythe and whettin-stane
– or bill or heuk nou I mind the words.
And cuttin new gress for pounies owre in the field.
And boontree canes – for bows and arrows.'
The gullion for takin out the powny on a halter
for special grazin when it's dried out. The gullion
for cuttin fails.

I can mind the gullion wi the swings
and muckle puddles for jumpin. And the stane dyke
for settin up tin cans for shootin at
wi a point two five – I think. And the speugies
and stookies and craws – and blackies e'en.
And waas to sclim to fields for shootin
foxes – ae fox – and maukins and rats. And huntin
out peeweeps' eggs or stanein wasps' bike
– and rinnin for the gullion.

I can mind the gullion and aa the lans ayont.
I went back and fund
a wee bit boggy grund.

STRANGER IN TOUN

You being frae Fife and born in Mallaig
I took you to see my Glasgow. The warm
humanity o' Argyle Street and the distinctive
smell o' the Subway. The haill lang length
o Sauchiehall Street and a quick visit
to the Mitchell Library and my first seat o' learnin'
at the table near the back. I took you for a walk
on Glasgow Green and into the People's Palace.
We stood by Clyde at the Broomielaw
and I spoke o' steamers for Doun the Watter
and happy holidays at the Fair.
We went on tramride to the Art Gallery
and I stood wi' you afore Rembrandt's
A Man in Armour. We had time
to haud haunds lookin out to the country
frae the heichts o' the University and stood
quait in the nave o' the auld Cathedral. I showed
you Barlinnie Prison and the closes o' daurkest Coucaddens
and the seikness o' the Gorbals. We had a seat
in the sun in George Square wi' its mony statues

and there was much Victoriana to be seen
afore high tea in famous Glasgow tea-room.
We had the best seats in Alhambra
Theatre for pantomime wi' real Glasgow
comedians at the day's end.

Being frae Fife and born in Mallaig
you said,
'I liked the Rembrandt.'

NOON

Midsummer day and picnicking at noon.
In the meadow lands
on the upper fields there are buttercups in bloom.
And you like butter
and cream.
And your hair lang and spread out on the gress.
And me gaitherin it in my haunds
and kept for aye in my mind.

ANDREW GREIG

Andrew Greig was born in Bannockburn, Stirling, in 1951.
Educated at Waid Academy, Anstruther, and Edinburgh University
(Philosophy). Now a full-time writer. Part-time climber on three
Himalayan mountaineering expeditions. E C Gregory Award 1972;
Writer-in-residence at Glasgow University in 1979–81; Scottish-
Canadian Exchange Fellow 1982–83. Five poetry collections and
two Himalayan expedition books.

Because like ourselves they make fuller sense in the context of their
friends-and-relations, I have not selected any poems from the quasi-
narratives of *Men On Ice* or *A Flame In Your Heart*.

'The Maid & I' still pleases me and is representative of certain
natural tendencies in my writing. My natural voice seems to be a
lyric one with an underlying four-stress unit, guided by
considerations of sound and the tone of a speaker rather than by
more evident formal structures. This poem is also characteristic in
talking about two things at the same time – not precisely metaphor
and certainly not symbolism.

I am interested in a poetry that explores – reports on – unusual areas
of experience. 'Interlude on Mustagh Tower' is a moment in time
from my first Himalayan climbing expedition.

After twenty years developing one's 'natural voice', it can become
necessary ('to find what will suffice') to go beyond or disrupt it.
Phillip Hobsbaum talks about the transition from 'songs' to 'poems'
– perhaps that is why I now find myself interrupting and subverting
my own tendencies. Much of the evident musicality is stripped out.
The poem becomes more dissonant, more compressed; the voice
more direct yet more evidently involved in artifice. I see poems now
as inhabiting the tension between natural voice and imposed form.
This aesthetic and the subject matters (crudely, the personal and the
social-political) of the two 'Screwed Sonnets' here, 'Heart & Irish'
and 'Last Pibroch In South Queensferry', form my present
preoccupations.

THE MAID & I

It's nothing personal when she slips in
at half-dawn, half-dusk, any drifting
time of day, to make mere solitude complete.
That's how come we get on
so well, so long. You smile, you picture
black-seamed stockings, white muslin crown,
hair that's dying to be let down? No,
she is not Naughty Lola –
nor Mrs Mopp! With us it is
importunate to talk or stare;
touch is right out. This fortunate
proximity is all we share.

She has arrived.
You are in the backroom,
by the Steinway, fiddling with the Blues.
You hear her humming as she moves
among the papers and abandoned meals, clearing up
the ashtrays, scripts and coffee cups,
the litter of aloneness. Redeeming fingers touch
your old scores lightly, as if it were yourself
she dusts and settles on the shelf. Praise the maid
who sets out flowers and white clouds
where you might see them and be glad!
The shambles would be total were it not for her.

Now she is singing an old refrain
you can't quite . . . The sky
is pale, washed clean by rain,
hung up against the evening.
As you attend, a melody floats
through apartment walls so intimately
it is as though you quote yourself –
debris is sorted, order
is invented or restored.
Now she is done. You will work on alone
but that's all right. Grace must have its means.
Her grave fingers switch on darkness as she leaves.

INTERLUDE ON MUSTAGH TOWER

In these high places we are melting out
of all that made us rigid; our ice-screws
hang loose on the fixed ropes to the Col.
Monday in the Himalaya, the clouds are down,
our objective is somewhere, but obscure –
let it soar without us for a day!
We lounge in thermals on the glacier,
brewing and shooting the breeze, that improbable
project of conversation among the living.
Laughter rings across the ice. Why not?
None of us will die today – that's immortality
you can drawn on in a cigarette,
sweet and harsh, the way we like it.
Steam rises from the billy, Sandy pours.
It is true high, worked for, that we pass
hand to hand between us with our brews.
Men on ice, going nowhere and laughing
at everything we cannot see but know
is there – among the cloud, on the Col,
a hand of some sort is tightening our screws.

HEART & IRISH

Your man's been ambushed by a holiday near Cork
years back with lady, Paud & Anne
with ½ acre marijuana and desire for children.
Peace broke out for days on end, fat pork
and laughter, winning at the dartboard & love . . .

With such memory, bent on re-uniting
or at least revenge (the unequal parting),
no peace for heart & Irish, no finis
to the troubles. On TV, the funeral

wants blood; Mum looks up, 'There's aye one
who kisses, one who's kissed.' Who wins
the struggle? Whoever dares
needs it less. Anyway, the vehicle's doomed
when a man squats on the roof and lets rip.

LAST PIBROCH IN SOUTH QUEENSFERRY

Enough fourteen-bar compressed & gurgling
pibrochs to you, Annie, whoever you were
(I mythed you). There are affairs
more pressing than love, say they who have it.

So look around. The bookie's satellite disc
shines on the new deli; library hours are cut;
my neighbour's roof leaks into mine
(would we were separate, or one) . . .

The Chancellor parks his belly on TV,
Auld Scotia is a bag of wind
in History's oxter. Beyond my town
the fields are burning, it is time to leave.

Rush hour. The trucks point North and whine,
the low sun splits the Road Bridge like a reed.

HAMISH HENDERSON

Hamish Henderson. Born Blairgowrie, 1919. Served in North Africa, Sicily and Italy with 51st Highland Division, and other infantry divisions. Liaison with Italian partisans. Published *Ballads of World War II* (1947) and *Elegies for the Dead in Cyrenaica* (1948: Somerset Maugham Award 1949). Joined newly founded School of Scottish Studies 1951; discovered Jeannie Robertson 1953. Translated Gramsci's *Prison Letters:* second (enlarged) edition 1988.

One of my chief loves has always been the anonymous song-poetry of Scotland, in both Scots and Gaelic. While in the army I composed several songs for the troops, one of which ('Banks of Sicily') really caught on, and turned into a kind of folksong.

Another permanent interest of mine has been the various lingos of the 'underworld', and of minority cultures generally; slang can often by its very nature get more ingeniously under the skin of a group or community than can a literary language of 'respectable' antecedent. The cant of the Scots travelling folk, which in some areas has invaded the local Doric, is the one I have drawn on in 'Floret Silva Undique'.

This line occurs in a medieval goliardic poem, and I have interwoven throughout lines from the marvellous English anonymn 'The bailey beareth the bell away', a superb example of the magical effect which can sometimes be engendered by the free flow of oral transmission.

Folksong can often treat the comedy of sex with a much surer touch than 'literary' poetry, and the eloquent tender rumbustious bawdry of the Scots anonymns is second to none in this respect. Fusing these various elements together, I have done my best to create a unified poem in celebration of 'Sexy May in Auld Reekie'.

'The Freedom Come-All-Ye' is a product of the Scottish folksong revival; it was composed for CND demonstrators in 1960. In it I have tried to express my hopes for Scotland, and for the survival of humanity on this beleaguered planet.

FLORET SILVA UNDIQUE

Floret silva undique
The lily, the rose, the rose I lay.

Tell-tale leaves on the elm-tree bole:
Reekie's oot for a Sabbath stroll.
Tim and Eck from their pad in Sciennes –
Cowboy T-shirts and Brutus jeans.
Gobstopper Gib and Jakie Tar
Billies oot the Victoria Bar
And Davie Bowie plyin' his trade
The sweetest minstrel was ever laid.
Floret silva undique
The rocker, the ring and the gowans gay.
The bonniest pair ye iver seen
Play chasie on the Meedies green.
Undressed to the nines, frae tit tae toe,
The kimmers o' Coogate are a' on show.
Ripper o' flies, lord o' the tools,
Yon mental boot boy Eros rules.

Floret silva undique
We'll hae a ball, though the Deil's to pay.
The quick and the slaw are game for a tear;
Sma'back snooves from his Greyfriars lair.
Out of the darkmans the queer coves come,
Janus guisers from bield and tomb.
Scrunchit hurdies and raw-bone heid
Junkies mell wi' the livin deid.
Get stuck in, Hornie, and show's the way.
The lily, the rose, the rose I lay.

Floret silva undique
The rockin' righteous are makin' hay.
Oot from their dens, as shair's your life,
Come Knox the poxy and Mac the knife;

Major Weir o' the twa-faced faith,
And Deacon Brodie in gude braid claith.
Seely sunshine and randy mirk
Like Auld Nick's wing ow'r a pairish kirk.
Whae's yon chattin' up Jess MacKay?
It's Bailie Burke, wi' his weet wall-eye.
The kinchin's bara, so clinch the deal:
Gie her a note, son, and hae a feel.
Edina – Reekie – mon amour.
Dae't, or I'll skelp your airse, ye hoor.
The flesh is bruckle, the fiend is slee
Susanna's elders are on the spree.
The bailie beareth the belle away.
The lily, the rose, the rose I lay.

Floret silva undique
Sweet on the air till dark of day.
Sma'back pipes and they dance a spring.
Over the grave all creatures sing.
The sun gangs doon under yon hill
Jenny and Jake are at it still.
To the greenwood must I go alas
Could you gie me a loan o Balaam's ass?
Alano I dig you the most.
The lily I laid, the rose I lost.
Whit dae ye hear amang the broom?
Spreid your thies, lass, and gie me room.
Twa gaed tae the woods, and three cam hame
Reekie, tell me my true love's name.
Edinburgh castle, toun and tour
The gowans gay and the gilliefloor.
Luvers daffin' aneath the slae
Floret silva undique
The bonniest pair ye iver seen
Fuckin' aneath the flooerin' gean.
Bairnies wankin' abuin the clay
Floret silva undique

Flora is queen of lusty May.
The lily, the rose, the rose I lay.

(from *Auld Reekie's Roses*)

Glossary: *Floret silva undique* – The wood is flowering all about; *billies* – chums; *gowans* – daisies; *kimmers* – girls; *Sma'back* – Death; *darkmans* – night (travellers' cant); *bield* – shelter; *scrunchit hurdies* – thin wizened buttocks; *mell* – mingle; *seely* – blessed, lucky; *The kinchin's bara* – the child is good (i.e. willing)   (travellers' cant); *gean* – cherry tree

THE FREEDOM COME-ALL-YE

(Tune: The Bloody Fields of Flanders)

Roch the wind in the clear day's dawin
    Blaws the cloods heelster-gowdie ow'r the bay,
But there's mair nor a roch wind blawin
    Through the great glen o' the warld the day.
It's a thocht that will gar oor rottans
    – A' they rogues that gang gallus, fresh and gay –
Tak the road, and seek ither loanins
    For their ill ploys, tae sport and play.

Nae mair will the bonnie callants
    Mairch tae war when oor braggarts crousely craw,
Nor wee weans frae pit-heid and clachan
    Mourn the ships sailin' doon the Broomielaw.
Broken faimlies in lands we've herriet
    Will curse Scotland the Brave nae mair, nae mair;
Black and white, ane til ither mairriet,
    Mak the vile barracks o' their maisters bare.

So come all ye at hame wi' Freedom,
    Never heed whit the hoodies croak for doom.
In your hoose a' the bairns o' Adam
    Can find breid, barley-bree and painted room.
When Maclean meets wi's friens in Springburn,
    A' the roses and geans will turn tae bloom,
And a black boy frae yont Nyanga
    Dings the fell gallows o' the burghers doon.

KATHLEEN JAMIE

Left school in 1979, wanting to be a writer. Two years of a vaguely leftist vegetarian lifestyle, and I went to university to read philosophy. Three collections of poetry, a radio play and an unpublished novel later, I almost dare call myself a writer. Still leftist, not vague, failed vegetarian.

I have chosen 'Child with Pillar Box and Bin Bags' because it's my most recent poem. A week after its writing I moved out into the country, so that's probably the last inner-city poem for a while. What is it about? Something to do with poverty, love, the government and their endless banging on about freedom of choice. This poem illustrates well of one of the forms my work takes (there are about four, I think). That listing, piling, litanising way of writing, with many concealed and half rhymes, I find suspiciously quick and easy. This poem took two or three drafts: two days' work.

'Hagen and the Owls at Glencoe'. That religious bent again. This is a recent poem. Hagen was a beloved house-cat, who died, and the poem has something of the way the transcendental supports and occasionally shines through the empirical, if I may put it thus.

'Julian of Norwich' took a year and a half and is, to my mind, the most interesting and hard-wrung poem I've done. Unlike 'Child with Pillar Box and Bin Bags', it doesn't refer to anything I've seen or experienced. I *respect* this poem, partly because I know how deep I had to delve for it. Its cool, accepting, weak-but-strong voice is one I wish I could hear again.

Travel so affects my writing I had to put in a travel-piece. 'The Wave Breaks' . . . for no other reason than that it's short.

CHILD WITH PILLAR BOX AND BIN BAGS

But it was the shadowed street-side she chose
while Victor Gold the bookies basked
in conquered sunlight, and though
Dalry Road Licensed Grocer gloried and cast
fascinating shadows she chose
the side dark in the shade of tenements;
that corner where Universal Stores' (closed
for modernisation), blank hoarding blocked
her view as if that process were illegal;
she chose to photograph her baby here,
the corner with the pillar box.
In his buggy, which she swung to face her.
She took four steps back, but
the baby in his buggy rolled toward the kerb.
She crossed the ground in no time
it was fearful as Niagara,
she ran to put the brake on, and returned
to lift the camera, a cheap one.
The tenements of Caledonian Place neither
watched nor looked away, they are friendly buildings.
The traffic ground, the buildings shook, the baby breathed
and maybe gurgled at his mother as she
smiled to make him smile in his picture;
which she took on the kerb in the shadowed corner,
beside the post-box, under tenements, before the
bin bags hot in the sun that shone
on them, on dogs, on people on the other side
the other side of the street to that she'd chosen,
if she'd chosen or thought it possible to choose.

HAGEN AND THE OWLS AT GLENCOE

There's a touch of the witch,
a shaft of God between clouds
a death in the house, and life
is a cobweb of glass.

The cat's buried at the river,
his death weighs like water in a sack
the owls that cry in the night-time
dropped us a mouse with no back.

Such things by the door in the morning!
things to keep you knowing
that God is in the potting shed,
puts your eyes to a crack between slats.

JULIAN OF NORWICH

Everything I do, I do for you
Brute. You inform the dark
inside of stones, the winds draughting in

from this world and that to come,
but never touch me.
You took me on

but dart like a rabbit into holes
from the edges of my sense
when I turn, walk, turn.

I am the hermit whom you keep
at the garden's end, but I wander.
I am wandering in your acres

where every step, were I
attuned to sense them,
would crush a thousand flowers.

(Hush, that's not the attitude)
I keep prepared a room and no-one comes.
(Love is the attitude)

Canary that I am, caged and hung
from the eaves of the world
to trill your praise.

(He will not come.)
Poor bloodless hands, unclasp.
Stiffened, stone cold knees, bear me up.

(And yet, and yet, I am suspended
in his joy, huge and helpless
as the harvest moon in a summer sky.)

THE WAVE BREAKS . . .

The wave breaks on the smallest stone,
rolls on. Dawn as eternal occurrence;
always someplace. Darkness, dusk, day,
seem immutable as the poplar trees
that make a place. It's permanent
midnight at that check-point, or where
the herd and goats turned to stare
forever half-light, soft as chicks.
Unmanned border of night and day, we rumble on
toward the sun – a tiny cut in orange peel,
sharp sting of smell – Ah, breakfast!

ROBERT ALAN JAMIESON

I was born in Shetland in 1958. I've published one collection of poetry (*Shoormal*) so far, as well as two short novels. More recently I've been writing for stage. I live at present in Queensferry, with Wilma and our two young sons, while studying English and Philosophy at the University of Edinburgh.

These two poems mark the beginning and the end of a certain process of thought which occupied the poet in me over a number of years, from late adolescence into early maturity. During this time I was concerned primarily with the flux of language which contained somewhere a definition of that poet – Shetlandic, Scots and English all used me in a different way. These poems are chronologically the extremes of the sequence published as *Shoormal*: a Shetlandic word for the shallows on a beach, the tidal area; a word which I latterly discovered to have the metaphorical sense of 'a dilemma'.

I think it interesting that in 'My Father's Life', written when I was nineteen, I was used by the most alien tongue of the three, the learned English, in dealing with a subject which was specifically local and personal – as if I needed some displacement in order to voice these feelings at all. Eight years later, the final poem in the sequence, 'Glowerin at da Mune, Lichtin ida Midden', was written in a variety of Shetlandic strange even to modern speakers of the dialect, because of the use of forgotten Norn (Norse) words. The subject – a flyte upon the inadequacy of the free market/state control antithesis as a means of economic governance – was again handled obliquely by this principle of displacement.

Looking at these poems as some sort of origination and destination, I see the journey more clearly than I might have done if I had considered every turning step I made along the way. I feel at ease, now, in my dilemma.

MY FATHER'S LIFE

In the car, I hear the next
Installment of the sickness.
Jimmy and Betty, sister and brother,
Their eighty years of independence ended,
As the district nurse efficiently
Opens up their private drawers
And packs a little bag.

Into a spotless disinfected
Iron bedstead home; in short,
they have relinquished soul
Beneath the agonising affliction of age.

My father tells the tale
with proper, sober, laconic
pithy pity, labouring against
the potential resignation
in his eye (I see it).

All around him is this sickness, creeping,
As the village suddenly decides it's time to die.
As the sickle swipes another two or three
and lays them horizontal, as the ripened corn.

As he drives he has the look of a man
Whose faith is rapidly deserting him.
My early memories recall him wilful, strong, decisive.
Now he seems strained.

I think that grief must be the lather
which emotion rubs from sorrow,
so dispersing it.
I think my father holds the last tight
fingered grip against emotion,
and that his sorrow
is a deep felt solid longing
for that which has passed.

GLOWERIN AT DA MUNE, LICHTIN IDA MIDDEN

At da hert o aa tocht lies
A geometry o shapes o things
Dat never come, but fir aa dat
Ir skabilaas dat nomen fok'll
Wirk on trang t'rekk an bigg.

Dey tak nae ru, quhile i dir
Heads da trines o graand dimensions
Shest dem sam as dey wir bitten
Be da frøtt dat if dey could but
Raise it up, dan aa da powre

Athin its midst wid be da
Key t'every powre, an aa gods
O aa erts, an herts, wid bide
Tagidder in a single shalter
Sharin wan unholy name.

Standin dan apo dis stab,
Glinderin up trowe modrin mirk
O man-made cloods an shilpit-rain,
Believin' still da ladder gait o'
Black, quhite, red an gowden steps

Can lift dem up abøn da
Elt o human misery, lowse fae
Da chow o da mooth's demands,
Maet dram, pipe or tittie, solace fir
Da bairn ootgrown da bosy,

Glowerin at da mune, dey
Dønna see dat quhile dir vargin on
T'mak baest saint, da base da pure,
Anidder gadderie o fok ir
Klekkin on t'tak fae aa

An gie t'ane or twartree
Aa forbye da peeriest puckle,
Da hidmist skitlin, token vote,
Athoot a tocht amid dir skelkin
Fir bairns wi bellies swalled

Fir want o mael an watter,
Athoot a tocht o hoo da suddren
Fremd ir deein, rigabens',
Or Aert herself grown dowd an pøshnis,
Her blød sookt o its pooster.

At da hert o dis onkerry
Is da forken mooths o dem dat hae
Enyoch an mair, but irna blaet
T'rekk an tak fae dem dat irna
Aeten, nor yit even boarn!

An laek da idder fok, dem
Sea aaber ida biggin o dir
Skabilaas, dir glowerin at
Da mune an lichtin ida midden,
Heids ida air, shøn ida sharn.

Glossary of words outwith the *Concise Scots Dictionary: ir, irna* – are, are not; *skabilaa* – impractical dream; *nomen* – intelligent; *trang* – preoccuppied; *rekk* – reach; *ru* – rest; *frøtt* – superstition; *apo* – upon; *stab* – a sea rock; *glinder* – to peer; *trowe* – through; *shilpit* – acidic; *elt* – a jumble; *bosy* – bosom; *dønna* – do not; *gadderie* – a gathering; *klekk* – to swarm; *peerie* – small; *skelkin* – mocking laughter; *fremd* – strangers; *rigabens* – a bony creature; *pøshnis* – poisonous; *forken* – greedy; *blaet* – shy, timid; *aaber* – keen, eager; *ida* – in the; *shøn* – shoes

NORMAN KREITMAN

Norman Kreitman is a doctor working in medical research in Edinburgh, where he has lived for over twenty years. He resumed writing poetry after a long interval, and published some of his recent work in *Touching Rock* (Aberdeen University Press) in 1987. A second volume of poems is awaiting publication.

The choice of these three poems is quite arbitrary, or so it seems to me. But evidently I have retained a certain interest in them, and conceivably some of my present notions about them may interest the reader.

'St Chrystobole' was an early poem arising from the observation that people engaged in heroic work of great significance may nevertheless flag in their efforts through the monotony of their routine; single-mindedness is a great cause of boredom.

'Excluded by Mountains' has philosophical pretensions but is essentially an attempt to explore the sheer stubbornness of the world around us and the indifference of matter to human concerns. The question of the 'otherness' of Nature, alternating with its 'closeness', is one which I find fascinating, though few contemporary poets appear to share my concern.

'Designing a Japanese Garden' tries to use the alien conventions of an exotic culture as a means of seeing afresh our own needs for and use of personal space. And, of course, it is not just in connection with gardens that we wilfully exclude what we all agree to be important in favour of the trivial.

ST CHRYSTOBOLE

'Thy fires, Lord, which blazing rim
the fierce horizon of the world.
Thy nails of pain extend each limb,
define the human form, teaching us
open-armed embrace of Your loss.'

St Chrystobole rose from bleeding knee,
took up his book and from the wall
a wooden cross to goad his journey,
went to seek out unending pain
to learn to celebrate its name.

He chose to dwell among cactus blades
by the rocks at the tawny desert's edge.
Through the years he every moment prayed,
eyes tightly shut in a wilderness
of sand and grief and his distress.

But slowly, in that nameless place,
the ache grew less compelling;
as one who construes a familiar face
attention flickered, and what he sought
would slip aside in a drifting thought.

Heat bent his head and stilled his psalm.
The desert mice observed wide-eyed
how against the stump of a withered palm
St Chrystobole, that godly one,
sat dozing in the evening sun.

EXCLUDED BY MOUNTAINS

We have always believed in mountains,
their inwardness, and how they ascend
to perimeters of blue; high lords they are.

Their heads are always turned away,
their thoughts ruthless. Consider the essence
of stone, how men dying of thirst

will suck a pebble yet still go mad,
their senses unweighted. Reflect how the prophet
on finding truths as certain as flint

discovers them more obdurate than his own despair.
And how little the hand achieves on squeezing,
hard, even smallest grit, and bleeds on separation.

So do not expect, but extend your arm, touch
with most careful fingertips this huge rock,
and feel the cold surface of a great god's back.

DESIGNING A JAPANESE GARDEN

First you must ask disturbing questions;
do you, for example, insist on walking about
   or have you acquired
enough understanding to stay in one place?

Then consider purpose. Presumably the garden
will chiefly be used for poetry competitions,
   or will you drink tea,
or instead, think of the verities of the Masters?

Decide next on what is within, what is out,
how light shall enter the eye of the house
   when shadows lean outwards,
where the floor will end and the world begin.

And clarify your thoughts concerning the open air;
need you borrow space from the hazy mountains
   or is the nearer sky enough?
Would a wall help to block and organise your seeing?

Then you may set your garden, but choose to show
chiefly those truths which are assymetrical;
   pain need not appear
but have water for balm, rushes for consolation.

   Finally, place the massive stone,
   and let that be your gravity.

EDDIE LINDEN

Born in Ireland in 1935 and brought up in Lanarkshire. Educated at the Holy Family School, Mussend, Bellshill. Left school at fifteen, worked as a coalminer, then a steelworker. Won a scholarship at the age of twenty-nine to Plater College, Oxford, where I studied Economics for three years. Founded the literary magazine, *Aquarius,* in 1968, and it has reached the eighteenth issue. Subject of a biography by Sebastian Barker, *Who is Eddie Linden?* (1979). In 1980 a collection of poems, *City of Razors,* was published.

The poems in this selection have been chosen because, apart from being the ones to which I feel closest, they seem to appeal more strongly to others. They also reflect the range of my social concerns which I feel is an important aspect of my work. Inevitably, in a body of work that deals with people, these concerns sometimes become more intimate.

PRAYERS FOR THE FOETUS

(for Gavin Ewart)

Thanks for inviting me to your table
Surrounded by the instruments of the Catholic Church
And that nun resenting the lady that had an abortion
And they all talked about the prayer meetings
And how much hot tea was given at the door.
The sacrifice of the mass
And the prayers for the foetus thrown in the bin
And then he said 'Go in peace'
And the altar boy had an erection
And the mass was over
And the supper was over
And they picked up the baby and took it home.

THE SLUM

There's not much sun ever gets through
Winter or summer
The roof is cracked
And the wall oozes its continuous sweat
A worm is worming her way through life
She's only thirty
With the unborn inside –
Seems to have been on the move
From one den to another:
Ten years in a dirt-box, and the little animals
Have never seen a bath.
It always rains, inside and outside.
Her life goes on,
Waiting for the day when the door will open
And the sun will shine –
Not as long as that bastard's on the door-knob.
The mean street with ragged children
Dog-shit and broken glass.
The fuzz crawling around
As if protecting the slums.
At night they clear the air with violence.
Beer helps to forget the mess.
Then there's the Negro boy. He starts to thunder,
With much the same self-pity.
They can't see they're in the same boat
In this hungry palace
Full of hungry faces,
Objects waiting to be delivered
From this dump, and moved
Into a larger dump,
That's far too steep to look down.
Much colder than the pavements they left twelve
    months ago.

CITY OF RAZORS

(for the City of Glasgow)

Cobbled streets, littered with broken milk-bottles,
reeking chimneys and dirty tenement buildings,
walls scrawled with FUCK THE POPE and
   blue-lettered
words GOD BLESS THE RANGERS.
Old woman at the corner, arms folded, babe in pram,
a drunk man's voice from the other pavement,
And out come the Catholics from evening
   confessional;

A woman roars from an upper window
'They're at it again, Maggie!
Five stitches in our Tommy's face, Lizzie!
Eddie's in the Royal wi' a sword in his stomach
and the razor's floating in the River Clyde.'

There is roaring in Hope Street,
They're killing in the Carlton,
There's an ambulance in Bridgeton,
And a laddie in the Royal.

DRAG SHOW

Walking through a lonely bar
Full of hungry faces.
On stage she danced
through a sea of smoke.
While men mocked and laughed
at her act. Her eyes told
you everything.
Pain that travelled through
every vein with dead music
and cheap jokes.

A TABLE OF FRUIT

(for Fr Michael Hollings)

Your table contains everything.
You and everyone share Christ.
Faith and prayer are part of the day.
Time and space are made possible.
Nothing will distract you from your purpose or plans
Even when you are not there.

Quiet are your ways
But your message gets through.
Your trees bear fruit.
You see to your garden in a practical way,
Nor do you harrass your workers,
Only guide their hands.

Everything is carefully placed in time
For Mass; when they arrive you will be there
Carrying the bread and wine.

A SUNDAY IN CAMBRIDGE

(For William)

That Sunday was like an unfinished dream.
I've never been able to get it out of my mind.
You looked like Mary Magdalen
And I wanted to wash your feet.
The more I looked into your eyes
The stronger the pain.
Your thin body and small waist
Were all I wanted to possess
But a shadow hovering in our midst
Prevented a possible communion.

MAURICE LINDSAY

Born Glasgow, 1918. Trained as musician. After war service, music critic and broadcaster; Programme Controller, Border Television 1961; Director, The Scottish Civic Trust 1967–83. Married, one son, three daughters. Lives Milton Hill, Dumbarton. Books include: *History of Scottish Literature; The Burns Encyclopaedia; Collected Poems* (1979); *A Net to Catch the Wind; The French Mosquitoes' Woman* and *Requiem for a Sexual Athlete.*

I sometimes wonder why anyone bothers to write poetry. It is an unfashionable and unprofitable art, a fact brought home to me, not so long ago, 'In a Glasgow Loo'

> Ah hope yuh dinna mind me speaking tae yi,
> sur, but ahve seen youse on the telly? Whit dyuh dae
> for a livan? Yuv retired? Yuh wrote? Apo-it?
> Micht ye no jist as weel hae peed inti thuh wund?

Perhaps, like that celebrated character who, whenever the urge to take exercise assailed him, lay down until the feeling passed off, poets might be wise to follow a similar course. Throughout my life, however, I have responded in verse to the troublings that impel the lyric cry. As a poet for the most part celebrating dailyness – 'he makes the mundane marvellous', one kindly critic observed – my themes tend to be drawn from everyday life. I have chosen 'Aged Four' and 'At the Mouth of the Ardyne' as illustrations of this concern; 'At Hans Christian Andersen's Birthplace, Odense, Denmark' and 'Anon' because they comment from different viewpoints on the problem of personal identity. Even the places we loved best in childhood do not stay for our comfort; hence 'Toward Light'. I have included one late poem, 'The Vietnam Memorial, Washington DC', my response to a twentieth-century dilemma too complex for the conventionally opposed appropriations of either Marxists or militarists. In the end it, too, comes back to the simple human values of dailyness.

ANON

They are excavating the mound at the foot of the village,
young men with gentle eyes and curious beards,
and names like Brown and Soutar, and soft-breasted girls
on whom they'll one day stamp their borrowed image,
name upon name. What else have they to preserve?

They are digging for signs. How like were the other Browns
and Soutars, ripening out of the blameless soil,
and having to leave their names when it took them under?
Turning over the freshly wounded earth,
only Anon stares out from whitened bone.

AT THE MOUTH OF THE ARDYNE

The water rubs against itself,
glancing many faces at me.
One winces as the dropped fly
Tears its tension. Then it heals.

Being torn doesn't matter.
The water just goes on saying
all that water has to say:
what the dead come back to.

Then a scar opens.
Something of water is ripped out,
a struggle with swung air.
I batter it on a loaf of stone.

The water turns passing faces,
innumerable pieces of silver.
I wash my hands, pack up, and go
home wishing I hadn't come.

Later, I eat my guilt.

AT HANS CHRISTIAN ANDERSEN'S BIRTHPLACE

Sunlight folds back pages of quiet shadows
against the whitewashed walls of his birthplace. Tourists
   move
through crowded antiseptic rooms and ponder
what row after row of glass-cased papers ought to prove.

Somehow the long-nosed gangling boy who was only
at home in fairyland, has left no clues.
The tinder-box of Time we rub
answers us each the way we choose.

For kings have now no daughters left for prizes.
Swineherds must remain swineherds; and no spell
can make the good man prince; psychiatrists
have dredged up wonder from the wishing well.

The whole of his terrible, tiny world might be
dismissed as a beautiful madman's dream, but that each of us
   knows
whenever we move out from the warmth of our loneliness
we may be wearing the Emperor's new clothes.

AGED FOUR

Alone beside himself, head-in-air
he wanders gently through a fading season,
almost for the last time aware
of how a moment feels, before the lesion

of growing into thought begin to hurt;
the falling burn turn into a complaint
it can't communicate; earth on the hands be dirt
that rubs a sudden scolding up; each feint

the wind boxes the trees with, trace a why
nobody answers; rain be more than wet;
clouds that unfold each other, shape a sky
forecasting portent. Head-in-air, and yet

reluctant to come in, he stands and bawls,
sensing from how much loss his mother calls.

TOWARD LIGHT

The distant fog-horns bicker, the near ones boom;
light bats across the ceiling of the room
where, forty years ago, I watched, awake;
a still unfocused schoolboy out to take
life by the meaning. Then, the mist that gripped
the perfumed garden, kept the sea tight-lipped,
hung vague on sheltering curtains; the boy's mind
compassed on ships whose fogs lay far behind.
Now, with the frame loose, the window bare,
a blunt beam's thrown back on its own stare.

THE VIETNAM MEMORIAL, WASHINGTON DC

Marshalled platoons of tourists troop to see
this gestured ceremonial public loss:
while peasants learn to live with what they must,
here, downed as if by flak, a grounded V
lies sunk in its uncastellated fosse,
staring its lists of bleak dismembered trust.

When menace leans beyond its emphasis
and leaders borrow lives to flesh their need
upholding the abstraction of a cause,
one side or the other comes to this.
The future cocks an ear that both must heed
if they would win posterity's applause,

claim cynics. But we know, less well-deceived,
the just can't always mollify their aims.
So the stone mourns the father, husband, son
in gleaming mindless glory, state-conceived,
while we mourn corporate numbers, not the names,
where some stand numbly, eyes only for one.

LIZ LOCHHEAD

Born Motherwell, Lanarkshire, 1947, trained in the Drawing and
Painting Department of Glasgow School of Art where she began
writing poems during the late 1960s. Published *Memo For Spring*
(her first collection) in 1972 which became a poetry bestseller. Lots
of poetry readings all over the UK and many in Canada, USA,
Austria, France and Germany. Since the early 1980s she has been
working increasingly in the theatre, particularly for the Royal
Lyceum Theatre, Edinburgh, and for the experimental/popular
Communicado Theatre Company which tours the UK and now
abroad. Her *Dreaming Frankenstein And Collected Poems* from
Polygon also includes 'Islands' (1978) and 'The Grimm Sisters'
(1981). Lives in Glasgow.

Why did I choose these poems? Because, I suppose, I must like
them the best. For reasons which are mostly obscure and
mysterious to me and – where they are not – are of no interest to
anybody but myself, although – naturally – I hope the poems
themselves are!

I know there is a special kind of excitement for me, and I'd be
willing to bet this is universally true for all writers, during those rare
and random times when a poem is 'coming about its own business'.
I may well have been – indeed I am very likely to have been – dull,
flat, stale, low, bored or lonely before a poem has decided to write
itself in me, through me, but as it emerges and I'm taking it down,
listening to it, tinkering with it, cutting out the bits that shouldn't
be in it, it is full of surprise and interest for me. Some more than
others, of course, and I remember these being particularly
surprising and satisfying to me. Even at the time. I wasn't proud of
them. How could I be? I didn't think they were clever either,
because they're not. They just seemed complete and quite separate
from me and not 'made up'. There they were. And I was glad to see
them.

WHAT THE POOL SAID, ON MIDSUMMER'S DAY

I've led you by my garrulous banks, babbling
on and on till – drunk on air
and sure it's only water talking –
you come at last to my silence.
Listen, I'm dark
and still and deep enough.
Even this hottest gonging sun
on this longest day
can't white me out.
What are you waiting for?
I lie here, inviting, winking you in.

The woman was easy.
Like to like, I called her, she came.
In no time I had her
out of herself, slipping on my water-stockings,
leaning into, being cupped and clasped
in my green glass bra.
But it's you I want, and you know it, man.
I watch you, stripped, knee-deep
in my shallows, telling yourself
that what makes you gasp
and balls your gut
is not my coldness but your own fear

– Your reasonable fear,
what's true in me admits it.
(Though deeper, oh
older than any reason).
Yes, I could
drown you, you
could foul my depths, it's not
unheard of. What's fish
in me could make flesh of you,
my wet weeds against your thigh, it
could turn nasty.

I could have you
gulping fistfuls fighting yourself
back from me.

I get darker and darker, suck harder.
On-the-brink man, you
wish I'd flash and dazzle again.
You'd make a fetish of zazzing dragonflies?
You want I should zip myself up
with the kingfisher's flightpath, be beautiful?
I say no tricks. I say just trust,
I'll soak through your skin and
slake your thirst.

I watch. You clench,
clench and come into me.

MY RIVAL'S HOUSE

is peopled with many surfaces.
Ormolu and gilt, slipper satin,
lush velvet couches,
cushions so stiff you can't sink in.
Tables polished clear enough to see distortions in.

We take our shoes off at her door,
shuffle stocking-soled, tiptoe – the parquet floor
is beautiful and its surface must
be protected. Dust
cover, drawn shade,
won't let the surface colour fade.

Silver sugar-tongs and silver salver
my rival serves us tea.
She glosses over him and me.
I am all edges, a surface, a shell

and yet my rival thinks she means me well.
But what squirms beneath her surface I can tell.
Soon, my rival
capped tooth, polished nail
will fight, fight foul for her survival.
Deferential, daughterly, I sip
and thank her nicely for each bitter cup.

And I have much to thank her for.
This son she bore –
first blood to her –
never, never can escape scot free
the sour potluck of family.
And oh how close
this family that furnishes my rival's place.

Lady of the house.
Queen bee.
She is far more unconscious,
far more dangerous than me.
Listen, I was always my own worst enemy.
She has taken even this from me.

She dishes up her dreams for breakfast.
Dinner, and her salt tears pepper our soup.
She won't
give up.

GEORGE MacBETH

I was born in Shotts, Lanarkshire, and went south with my father
and mother in 1935. We lived in Sheffield for many years, and
returned to Scotland for long holidays. My education has been in
England, but my sense of identity lies north of the border. I live
now in another country, beyond water, and regard myself as a
landowner and an exile.

I have chosen these three poems from my last book, *Anatomy of a
Divorce*, because they mark a return to an earlier style, and because
they seem true to the feelings they sprung from. It worries me, too,
that certain early poems are too often reprinted in anthologies,
acquiring a spurious familiarity and cachet through the laziness of
editors. A poet's own preference for his recent work may arise from
bias, a wish to resist the ageing process, for example; but at least he
has read his books. That said, one enjoys the support of a second
opinion, and there is little pride in herding forward verses others
have neglected. The poems here have been admired by friends
whose judgement I respect, and they come with that
recommendation, no other being of importance. As for being read
after one's death, I doubt if posterity should be spending time on
George MacBeth while there are still poets of the order of Sebastian
Evans to rediscover.

THE ADVENTURE

Was I set off one day walking
Carrying my heart. I went upstairs first
And there was a wash-hand basin, stinking cold,
Where someone threw it in, scrubbing
With a tough brush
Until it was clean. Well, it was clean

Before, I thought. So I took the back stairs
Down to the kitchen. There by the stove
Another one stood stirring a can of soup

In a saucepan. Fat spitting
Fell on my hands. Look out, he said,
Seizing me by the heart. Then he

Pitched it, all frozen as it was, hard
As a hamburger, into the
Boiling broth. So it sizzled, and softened.
Well, it was soft before. Soft enough,
I thought. But he said, no. No,
You say? Then I was tired. I

Took a turn down the corridor, slank
Through to the hall and up
The front stairs to bed. O, it was good
To lie down to rest my weary heart,
Then – ouch! There were thistles,
Tearing thistles, right out of Scotland's pride,

Burning the sheets. I felt my heart
Shrink at their touch. It bristled
And felt on fire. Well, it was hot
Enough before. A barrel of flame,
So it seemed to me. No, said a man
Standing there by the wardrobe

Setting shirts on a hanger. O, no.
Your heart was a dull old stick,
It needed stimulating. You see
The adventure is that you never know
How dirty and hard
Your heart is, or how ordinary,

Until one tries you. Be assured
You are wanted
When such trouble was gone to here
In your own subtle house
To commit your heart to these trials
Which it has come through so well. It shows

Your importance.

THE INQUISITION

Where were you last night?
Don't answer. I
Know where you were.

What was his name?
Don't answer. I
Know his name.

No, I don't want to know
Who you weren't with. When
I say you were
With someone, that's where you were.

Pass me the tongs.

You were where
I say you were, weren't you?
That's better.

Why were you there?
I know why, but I
Want to hear you say why.

The jug.
Swallow this.

Now tell me
Why you were where I don't
Want you to go.

Why you go there
With someone you know I don't want you to go with.

No, I don't want to know. I
Want to hear
The sound of my own voice going on and on.

Going on and on and on and on and on.

Tear out her tongue.

That's better.

THE CASKET

'Then Language, turning at the door,
Sent back one phrase, I love you,
To stay behind.

The Rolls was running, the chauffeur
Slapped his gloves at the wheel.

Sun glistened. A dazzling experience
Writing plays, being a screen writer's
Dream, awaited Language.
                              She nuzzled in furs,
Shifting her one jewel on a lean finger.

Then she handed it back. I love you,
Shines like a fragment of emerald
Now in my casket.
                              Outside
A storm nags, deep snow piles on the grating
Above the coal hole, the crows are asleep
In a wild cradle of difficulties.

Let Language go. Racing the moon
Across Europe to the valid, fresh capitals
Where men with canes are painting.
                              I am happy
With only three words to my name
In a little house echoing with reminiscence.

I bask in the glow
Surreptitious out of the sly velvet, the
Purples of enclosure where I have laid
My one jewel, a security against madness
And all the deaf energy of unrelenting time.

Be lucky, Language. Grow rich
In your own scenario, pocket millions.

One lurks here who remembers you.'
Thus dreamed
The carver of dumbbells, gliding
A pantoum by candlelight in his attic,
At a loss for words.

BRIAN McCABE

Brian McCabe was born in 1951 in Edinburgh. He studied
Philosophy and English Literature at the University of Edinburgh
and was awarded a Writer's Bursary by the Scottish Arts Council in
1980, since when he has lived as a freelance writer. His recent
publications are *The Lipstick Circus* (Mainstream) and *One Atom to
Another* (Polygon).

One of the things which first attracted me to poetry was the idea of
using a voice in a poem. I remember being impressed by Peter
Porter's 'Your Attention Please' and later by Edwin Morgan's uses
of voice. Most of my first poems played with the idea of the speaker
in some way, usually humorously, but as I wrote more I found out
that this could also be used dramatically. Exploring a voice is still
something I enjoy in poems, as many other poets do – perhaps it's
more central to contemporary Scottish poetry than to
contemporary English poetry? – and so I choose 'Noah' as an
example of this kind of poem.

My interest in voice has led me into the writing of radio drama and
some short stories in the form of monologue, but I think it's also led
me to think more about rhythm in poetry. I chose 'The Blind'
because I remembered that its rhythm was important – I wanted to
paint a picture, then make something happen in the picture, but to
do so I had to work the slow rhythm of what the poem was
describing into the lines.

I suppose simplicity is something I'm trying to achieve in some
poems, simplicity which isn't banality but more the residue of
statement you're left with when you've boiled off most of the
metaphor, if you're lucky. If you're unlucky, of course, you're left
with nothing at all, or too little. In 'The Seventh Sense' I felt that I
was left with enough.

NOAH

Don't talk to me of violence corruption
the imagination of man's heart and so forth
does not interest me I am a practical man
My inspirations come in cubits I deal in lists
of livestock fowl every creeping thing
I know of no Grace unless it is this
a talent for obedience for survival
Let me take a look at the blueprints
a window here a door there whatever
the specifications I will carry them out
to the letter Who am I to question
the merits of gopher wood the dimensions
or the destruction of all flesh No
my business is not to scan horizons
for that I use the raven the dove
If sacrifices are required I will make
sacrifices I have worked with animals
All will go in fear of me no matter
in the meantime my instructions are clear
be fruitful multiply I will do my part
replenish the earth leave it in my hands
A deluge so there will be a deluge
I am a family man I know nothing
of deluges I say nothing wish for nothing
but a quiet life perhaps a vineyard
I did not ask to be a prototype
So be it We have made our covenant.

THE BLIND

The blind old men who come arm in arm
On good-smelling days to the park,
Grateful to the girl who brings them
Since they seldom have the chance
Of a slow, recollective game of bowls.
The sun that signs their faces
With smudge-like marks where eyes were
Suggests to their memories a notion
Of green, and summer days ago.
Taking pleasure from the silence of grass
And the weight of the wood in the hand,
They engross themselves in the game
They play by sound intuition:
The girl is young, sighted.
She stands at the far end of darkness
And claps her hands – once, twice –
And then the first bowler stoops,
As if about to kneel and be blessed,
Then throws to her clapping hands.
As the dark wood is travelling the green
She waits, motionless, and waits
As if by any slight move she might alter
The swing and slowing of the bowl.
When it halts, she bows, she measures,
Then calls its distance, its 'time':
'Seven feet, at four o'clock.'
Again she claps her hands.
Another player stoops, lets go . . .
This time it comes closer, close enough
To enter the young girl's shadow
When it kisses the jack, there's a 'cloc'.

The old men smile.

THE SEVENTH SENSE

All talk of the Sixth
or of the Five
– none speak of the Seventh.

The Seventh sense can please itself
about what it apprehends:

the grey taste of a rainy day;
a premonition of an aroma;
what the caress once whispered
to a threadbare emotion.

The Seventh sense can dress
in whatever it can dream.

But like the moth who dreamt
she was an emperor
the Seventh sense is never very sure
that it exists.

That's why it keeps reminding us
– with the kiss of a snowflake,
with the colour of a shout –
that we do.

Who knows –
even the diligent earth
might forget to go on turning
if not for the Seventh sense.

NORMAN MacCAIG

Born in Edinburgh, 1910, but genetically I'm a Gael with a spoonful of Border blood slithering through my veins. I studied Classics at Edinburgh University and toiled (happily) as a teacher until I became Reader in Poetry at Stirling University. I am married, with two children and two grandchildren.

The earliest of these poems and the latest are separated by many years, though I don't know if any reader could put these few poems in chronological order. Is that a good thing or a bad? (The first book I admit to writing was published in 1955).

A place that matters very much to me includes Wester Ross and west Sutherland, and many of the things I write are situated there – and even when they're not, when they're about ideas or emotions, I find myself using images and metaphors, whose birthplace is in that beautiful landscape populated with, amongst other things, many of my closest friends.

I write about them, of course, one way or another. But other living creatures appear so frequently it would be stupid of me not to include an example, in this case 'Fetching Cows'.

'On the Pier at Kinlochbervie', a fishing village which has grown hugely since the occasion of this poem, is a rather unusual one for me. I'm not a moody fellow, but on that occasion I had an unpleasant sense of being separated, alienated from everything, even my own self. (It didn't last long.) The personal thing that now saddens me is the death of many of my closest friends and I write more about death than I used to. Not my own death. My view of that is Woody Allen's, who famously said he wasn't afraid of dying, he only wished he needn't be there at the time.

The poems are taken from *Collected Poems* (1985) and *Voice Over* (1988) both published by Chatto & Windus.

SMALL BOY

He picked up a pebble
and threw it into the sea.

And another, and another.
He couldn't stop.

He wasn't trying to fill the sea.
He wasn't trying to empty the beach.

He was just throwing away,
nothing else but.

Like a kitten playing
he was practising for the future

when there'll be so many things
he'll want to throw away

if only his fingers will unclench
and let them go.

SO MANY SUMMERS

Beside one loch, a hind's neat skeleton,
Beside another, a boat pulled high and dry:
Two neat geometries drawn in the weather:
Two things already dead and still to die.

I passed them every summer, rod in hand,
Skirting the bright blue or the spitting gray,
And, every summer, saw how the bleached timbers
Gaped wider and the neat ribs fell away.

Time adds one malice to another one –
Now you'd look very close before you knew
If it's the boat that ran, the hind went sailing.
So many summers, and I have lived them too.

ON THE PIER AT KINLOCHBERVIE

The stars go out one by one
as though a bluetit the size of the world
were pecking them like peanuts out of the sky's string bag.

A ludicrous image, I know.

Take away the gray light.
I want the bronze shields of summer
or winter's scalding sleet.

My mind is struggling with itself.

That fishing boat is a secret
approaching me. It's a secret
coming out of another one.
I want to know the first one of all.

Everything's in the distance,
as I am. I wish I could flip that distance
like a cigarette into the water.

I want an extreme of nearness.
I want boundaries on my mind.
I want to feel the world like a straitjacket.

SOUNDS OF THE DAY

When a clatter came
it was horses crossing the ford.
When the air creaked, it was
a lapwing seeing us off the premises
of its private marsh. A snuffling puff
ten yards from the boat was the tide blocking and
unblocking a hole in a rock.
When the black drums rolled, it was water
falling sixty feet into itself.

When the door
scraped shut, it was the end
of all the sounds there are.

You left me
beside the quietest fire in the world.
I thought I was hurt in my pride only,
forgetting that
when you plunge your hand in freezing water
you feel
a bangle of ice round your wrist
before the whole hand goes numb.

FETCHING COWS

The black one last as usual, swings her head
And coils a black tongue round a grass-tuft. I
Watch her soft weight come down, her split feet spread.

In front, the others swing and slouch; they roll
Their great Greek eyes and breathe out milky gusts
From muzzles black and shiny as wet coal.

The collie trots, bored, at my heels, then plops
Into the ditch. The sea makes a tired sound
That's always stopping though it never stops.

A haycart squats prick-eared against the sky.
Hay breath and milk breath. Far out in the West
The wrecked sun founders though its colours fly.

The collie's bored. There's nothing to control . . .
The black cow is two native carriers
Bringing its belly home, slung from a pole.

IN MEMORIAM

On that stormy night
a top branch broke off
on the biggest tree in my garden.

It's still up there. Though its leaves
are withered black among the green
the living branches
won't let it fall.

EWAN MacCOLL

Born 25 January, 1915 in Salford, Lancashire, to Scots parents.
Father an iron-moulder from Falkirk, mother from Auchterarder.
Left school on my fourteenth birthday. Various jobs and long spells
of unemployment. Worked in theatre – street theatre, experimental
groups – 1929–40. Theatre Workshop resident dramatist 1945–52.
Folksinger and songwriter since 1952.

'The Tenant Farmer'. Our cottage was in a frost-pocket as was his
farm. He was a man of few words. Even the Hogmanay dram didn't
loosen his tongue, at least not at first. It was during the third
Hogmanay that the pattern of silence was broken. We had been
singing bothy songs when he began to talk about his days as a farm-
servant; sheep, pigs and cattlebeasts, he had driven them all along
the old drovers' roads across Jock's Shoulder and Ettrick Pen and
down into Cumberland. I wrote 'The Tenant Farmer' and sang it to
him a year later. He didn't comment on it until he was leaving, then
he wrung my hand in both of his and said: 'Ay, that's how it was.'

'The Joy of Living'. The last time I climbed Suilven, or to be more
precise, failed to climb it, was in my seventy-second year. I was
with my wife and fourteen-year-old daughter Kitty. 'You go
ahead,' I told them, 'I'll meet you at the top.' But 'the flesh is
bruckle, the fiend is slee' and I hadn't gone more than half the
distance when my legs refused to carry me further. My body had
given me plenty of warnings over the last seven or eight years but
this was the final notice. My mountain days were over. I sat down
on a rock feeling utterly desolate. The feeling lasted for several days
and then my grief and sense of loss gave way to nostalgia and I
wrote 'The Joy of Living'. In an odd kind of way it helped me to
come to terms with my old age.

THE TENANT FARMER

My faither rented a piece o' land,
It was on the Carrick border;
And he spent damn near a' his fifty years
Tryin' tae get the land in order.
Snaw and hail and winter's gale,
He couldnae get nae rest,
He was just anither strugglin' tenant fairmer.

That wee bit fairm was ill tae wark,
It was coorse red clay and boulder,
But at blink o' day he'd be up the brae
Wi' the north wind at his shouther;
Plooin', sowin', reapin', hoein',
Wrestlin' wi' the clay.
He was jist anither daft-like tenant fairmer.

The land was choked wi' whin and dock,
And the broom it took some shiftin',
So he tore and chaved and he howked and slaved
At the pu'in and the liftin'.
Wark and sweat and rent and debt
And wife and bairns tae feed,
He was aye a weary, worried tenant fairmer.

Through the clay that turned in the coulter's trace
The young green corn cam' peepin',
And the barley thrived and the corn grew high,
And we a' helped wi' the reapin'.
August through and neeps tae pu',
There's aye a job tae dae
When you're a single-handed tenant fairmer.

But for a' the years o' his toil and sweat
And the never-ending battle,
He couldnae pay the bank ae day,
So they selt aff a' his cattle.

He damned the clay and cursed the day
That ever he warked the land,
The day that he became a tenant fairmer.

Well, whit wi' the cost o' the feedin' stuff
And the landlord's rent-increases –
They turned us oot and held a raup
O a' oor bits and pieces.
'Your fairm's ower sma', nae use at a'
And the owner needs the land;
Times are changed, we dinnae need a tenant fairmer'.

Noo he's warkin' on an assembly line,
It's a queer-like situation,
For he warks like hell makin' things that sell
For cash tae feed the nation.
It helps tae buy the corn and rye
And the kind o' crops he raised
When he was warkin' as a tenant fairmer.

THE JOY OF LIVING

Farewell you Northern hills, you mountains all, goodbye;
Moorland and stony ridges, crags and peaks, goodbye.
Glyder Fach farewell, Cul Beig, Scafell, cloud-bearing Suilven.
Sun-warmed rock and the cold of Bleaklow's frozen sea –
The snow and the wind and the rain on hills and mountains.
Days in the sun and the tempered wind and the air like wine,
And you drink and you drink till you're drunk on the joy of
living.

Farewell to you, my love, my time is almost done.
Lie in my arms once more until the darkness comes.
You filled all my days, held the night at bay, dearest companion.
Years pass by and are gone with the speed of birds in flight,
Our life like the verse of a song heard in the mountains.
Give me your hand then, love, and join your voice with mine,
We'll sing of the hurt and the pain and the joy of living.

Farewell to you, my chicks, soon you must fly alone,
Flesh of my flesh, my future life, bone of my bone.
May your wings be strong, may your days be long, safe be your
    journey.
Each of you bears inside of you the gift of love,
May it bring you light and warmth and the pleasure of giving;
Eagerly savour each new day and the taste of its mouth,
Never lose sight of the thrill and the joy of living.

Take me to some high place of heather, rock and ling,
Scatter my dust and ashes, feed me to the wind,
So that I will be part of all you see, the air you are breathing –
I'll be part of the curlew's cry and the soaring hawk,
The blue milkwort and the sundew hung with diamonds;
I'll be riding the gentle wind that blows through your hair,
Reminding you how we shared in the joy of living.

ALASTAIR MACKIE

Alastair Mackie, born Aberdeen 1925; took Hons degree in English, Aberdeen University 1950; taught at Stromness Academy and latterly Wade Academy; took early retirement 1983; awards from the Scottish Arts Council 1976, 1987. Now engaged in translations from Russian. Works: *Soundings* (Akros); *Clytach* (Akros); *Back-Green Odyssey* (Rainbow Books); *Ingaitherins* (AUP).

'I' the black dark': I chose this poem because it combines the sacred and profane and follows a Scots tradition of the intermingling of these two elements.

'Hand': I can't say why I selected this poem. It is unlike any other I've written. I can only guess it arose from remembering a sentence somewhere in the prose writings of the late MacDiarmid which I found particularly memorable. I have to paraphrase it. In between the thumb and index finger of the hand there is an area of skin which by its changing configurations is capable of registering a variety of emotional reactions. My poem, however, concentrates on the geography and functions of the hand rather than this interdigital space.

'Silences': This experience happened to me when the family were on holiday in Ardnamurchan some years back. It's actually taken from a Highland sequence. My reading of Baudelaire and Leopardi helped me to juxtapose my piece alongside two European figures whose silences stood in strong contrast to my own.

I' THE BLACK DARK

I' the black dark o the bedroom
the muckle ee o God –
Him that sees aathing –
looks doun
on twa bodies
his thooms drappit,
rib next rib.

Aipple ye are and
lang-leggit slidderie worm,
Eve-deil.
I straik your fruit,
skin whaur the serpent couers.
I tak the first bite,
Adam, dammt!

I'm smittit
wi the pest in ye.
I growe worm
and aipple baith.

He watches
twa worms touslin

Good or ill
we ken neither.

Like beasts,
beasts o the fields.

Wi the sweat o oor brous
we earn peace,
oor nicht-darg owre.

Swaalin ane anither
in oor book
is naebody's wyte.

Glossary: *pest* – pestilence; *touslin* – fondling each other; *nicht-darg*– night-work; *wyte* – blame

HAND

It's a delta o functions
aeons hae soopled.

And a map
runkled wi high-roads.

A cleuk forby
I share wi the beasts.

And a barescrape
wi a skiftin o hairs.

It has the face's weather,
its streetch o moods.

It can straik love
and thraw thrapples,

or be lowsed
in dreichness and soond sleep.

Its finger-nebs
snuff the skin o the world –

flouer, stane, wid, metal.
The things, oor neebors.

Brigs it maks
oot o handshaks.

Blinner than the een
it fichers in the dark

for the airt o things,
door-sneck or shouther bane.

When the condies o the body
stop their pumpin

the hands lie on the briest
cuddlin their tool-bags.

Glossary: *see facing page*

SILENCES

There is ae silence for Baudelaire,
whaur in the pit-mirk naethingness
is his grun in aa the airts
and he listens in for the wudness
souchin whiles thro his heid.
And ane for Leopardi
whaur frae the hill-tap
he picturs till himsel
thae silences abeen aa mortal ken
and the foonds o stillness
till aa thinkin fooners
and shipwrack is bliss in sic a sea.

Mine is mair hamely.
I sit on the ashet-rim o this broun pool,
its shallas fu o clood shapes and the lyft.
A Hieland coo stans stock-still
in its black seck of shadda.
I feel my heid gantin like a joug
that drap by drap fills up
wi aa the silence I could haud.
And syne when I was rim-fou
the spilth was skailt owre Ardnamurchan,
alang wi bools o sheep dirt, mussel shells,
the white keel o a seagull,
and the moors on their heathery mattress
sleepin soond.

Glossary: *wudness* – madness; *ashet-rim* – (the pool like) the edge of a broad dish; *lyft* – sky; *seck* – sack; *rim-fou* – brimful; *spilth* – overflow

Glossary: *soopled* – suppled; *runkled* – wrinkled; *cleuk* – claw-like hand; *barescrape* – barren land; *skiftin* – a light covering; *thraw* – twist; *thrapples* – throats; *lowsed* – loosened; *dreichness* – boredom; *finger-nebs* – finger tips; *fichers* – fumbles; *airt* – direction; *condies* – veins (literally pipes, conduits)

SORLEY MacLEAN
(SOMHAIRLE MacGILL-EAIN)

Sorley MacLean (Somhairle MacGill-Eain), born in Raasay in 1911, of a family of tradition-bearers, monoglot Gaelic speaker until he went to school. Taught in Skye, Mull, Edinburgh and Plockton. Wounded thrice in Libya and Egypt. Gave great help to teachers who were trying to save Gaelic in secondary schools, and hence in all schools.

I have chosen 'Hallaig' (written in 1952 or 1953) because I think it is at once intellectually comprehensive and welling from the sub-conscious, saying much implicitly about the history of our country and about the human condition, especially about time as it impinges on the human spirit. I think its image symbolism is original and spontaneous. I am told by many that it is complex and subtle, with a simplicity that gives what MacDiarmid has called 'a kything sight' of implicities. Also, I think it evokes landscape and history at the same time, and I hope it deserves what Dr John MacInnes has said about my poetry: 'living language. They are so Gaelic, so different from anything else in Gaelic, so different from anything else at all.'

I have chosen 'The National Museum of Ireland' (written in 1970) because it too has so much of history in it, so much of the tragic history of Scotland and of the world as well as of Ireland. A Gael, if he is at all a Gael, must love Ireland as well as Scotland, and as Ruskin has said, 'a soldier's job is not killing but to be killed, and I can think of no famous soldier who embodies as much as Connolly does my ideals of Gaeldom, socialism, heroism and martyrdom. I think that the metre is original in Gaelic, which is of some importance. I think that the very irregular rhymes of the first half of the poem lead on to a kind of climax in the more regular ones of the second half.

HALLAIG

'Tha tim, am fiadh, an coille Hallaig'

Tha bùird is tàirnean air an uinneig
triomh 'm faca mi an Aird an Iar
's tha mo ghaol aig Allt Hallaig
'na craoibh bheithe, 's bha i riamh

Eadar an t-Inbhir's Poll a' Bhainne,
thall 's a bhos mu Bhaile-Chùirn:
tha i 'na beithe, 'na calltuinn,
'na caorunn dhìreach sheang ùir.

Ann an Screapadal mo chinnidh,
far robh Tarmad's Eachunn Mór,
tha 'n nigheanan 's am mic 'nan coille
ag gabhail suas ri taobh an lóin.

Uaibhreach a nochd na coilich ghiuthais
ag gairm air mullach Cnoc an Rà,
dìreach an druim ris a' ghealaich –
chan iadsan coille mo ghràidh.

Fuirichidh mi ris a' bheithe
gus an tig i mach an Càrn,
gus am bi am bearradh uile
o Bheinn na Lice f' a sgàil.

Mura tig 's ann theàrnas mi a Hallaig
a h' ionnsaigh sàbaid nam marbh,
far a bheil an sluagh a' tathaich,
gach aon ghinealach a dh' fhalbh.

Tha iad fhathast ann a Hallaig,
Clann Ghill-Eain's Clann MhicLeoid,
na bh' ann ri linn Mhic Ghille-Chaluim:
Chunnacas na mairbh beò.

Na fir 'nan laighe air an lianaig
aig ceann gach taighe a bh' ann,
na h-igheanan 'nan coille bheithe,
direach an druim, crom an ceann.

Eadar an Leac is na Feàrnaibh
tha 'n rathad mór fo chóinnich chiùin,
's na h-igheanan 'nam badan sàmhach
a' dol a Chlachan mar o thùs.

Agus a' tilleadh as a' Chlachan,
á Suidhisnis 's á tir nam beò;
a chuile té òg uallach
gun bhristeadh cridhe an sgeòil.

O Allt na Feàrnaibh gus an fhaoilinn
tha soilleir an dìomhaireachd nam beann
chan eil ach coimhthional nan nighean
ag cumail na coiseachd gun cheann.

A' tilleadh a Hallaig anns an fheasgar,
anns a' chamhanaich bhalbh bheò,
a' lìonadh nan leathadan casa,
an gàireachdaich 'nam chluais 'na ceò,

's am bòidhche 'na sgleò air mo chridhe
mun tig an ciaradh air na caoil,
's nuair theàrnas grian air cùl Dhun Cana
thig peileir dian á gunna Ghaoil;

's buailear am fiadh a tha 'na thuaineal
a' snòtach nan làraichean feòir;
thig reothadh air a shùil 'sa choille:
chan fhaighear lorg air fhuil ri m' bheò.

HALLAIG

'Time, the deer, is in the wood of Hallaig'

The window is nailed and boarded
through which I saw the West
and my love is at the Barn of Hallaig,
a birch tree, and she has always been

between Inver and Milk Hollow,
here and there about Baile-chuirn:
she is a birch, a hazel,
a straight, slender young rowan.

In Screapadal of my people
where Norman and Big Hector were,
their daughters and their sons are a wood
going up beside the stream.

Proud tonight the pine cocks
crowing on the top of Cnoc an Ra
straight their backs in the moonlight –
they are not the wood I love.

I will wait for the birch wood
until it comes up by the cairn,
until the whole ridge from Beinn na Lice
will be under its shade.

If it does not, I will go down to Hallaig,
to the Sabbath of the dead,
where the people are frequenting,
every single generation gone.

They are still in Hallaig,
MacLeans and MacLeods,
all who were there in the time of MacGille Chaluim:
the dead have been seen alive.

The men lying on the green
at the end of every house that was,
the girls a wood of birches,
straight their backs, bent their heads.

Between the Leac and Fearns
the road is under mild moss
and the girls in silent bands
go to Clachan as in the beginning,

and return from Clachan
from Suisnish and the land of the living;
each one young and light-stepping,
without the heartbreak of the tale.

From the Burn of Fearns to the raised beach
that is clear in the mystery of the hills,
there is only the congregation of the girls
keeping up the endless walk,

coming back to Mallaig in the evening,
in the dumb living twilight,
filling the steep slopes,
their laughter a mist in my ears,

and their beauty a film on my heart
before the dimness comes on the kyles,
and when the sun goes down behind Dun Cana
a vehement bullet will come from the gun of Love;

and will strike the deer that goes dizzily,
sniffing at the grass-grown ruined homes;
his eye will freeze in the wood,
his blood will not be traced while I live.

ARD MHUSAEUM NA H-EIREANN

Anns na laithean dona seo
is seann leòn Uladh 'na ghaoid
lionnrachaidh 'n cridhe na h-Eòrpa
agus an cridhe gach Gàidheil
dh' an aithne gur h-e th' ann an Gàidheal,
cha d' rinn mise ach gum facas
ann an Ard Mhusaeum na h-Eireann
spot mheirgeach ruadh na fala
's i caran salach air en léinidh
a bha aon uair air a' churaidh
as docha leamsa dhiubh uile
a sheas ri peileir no ri béigneid
no ri tancan no ri eachraidh
no ri spreaghadh nam bom éitigh;
an léine bh' air O Conghaile
ann an Ard Phost-Oifis Eirinn
's e'g ullachadh na h-ìobairt
a chuir suas e fhéin air séithir
as naoimhe na 'n Lia Fail
th' air Cnoc na Teamhrach an Eirinn.

Tha an curaidh mór fhathast
'na shuidhe air an t-séithir,
ag cur a' chatha 'san Phost-Oifis
's ag glanadh shràidean an Dùn-Eideann.

THE NATIONAL MUSEUM OF IRELAND

In these evil days,
when the old wound of Ulster is a disease
suppurating in the heart of Europe
and in the heart of every Gael
who knows that he is a Gael,
I have done nothing but see
in the National Museum of Ireland
the rusty red spot of blood,
rather dirty, on the shirt
that was once on the hero
who is dearest to me of them all
who stood against bullet or bayonet,
or tanks or cavalry,
or the bursting of frightful bombs:

The shirt that was on Connolly
in the General Post Office of Ireland
while he was preparing the sacrifice
that put himself up on a chair
that is holier than the Lia Fail
that is on the Hill of Tara in Ireland

The great hero is still
sitting on the chair
fighting the battle in the Post Office
and cleaning streets in Edinburgh.

ADAM McNAUGHTAN

Adam McNaughtan was born in and, no matter his whereabouts, belongs to the East End of Glasgow. Educated at Whitehill School and Glasgow University, he has been teaching English since 1962, including two years in Scandinavia. His song-writing began in the late 1950s but has never been prolific. He prefers to publish in sound rather than in print.

I am a maker of songs. Much of my production is consciously ephemeral – rhymed accounts of occasions which are fresh in the memory of my listeners. The topicality and a close match of text and tune give pleasure to the audience. When the song is no longer topical much of the pleasure is lost.

The songs selected here arise not from passing events but from published and therefore permanent pieces of literature. Yet these songs represent different strands of my production.

'Oor Hamlet' is the more typical, from the somewhat laboured pun of the title onwards. The language, like the speech of most Glaswegians, is the local dialect salted with phrases from extraneous sources. The humour is largely verbal, from the outrageous rhymes to the reductive effect of the chosen language. (*cf.* Burns's reduction of bull-fighting to 'to fecht wi' nowte'.)

When I translate (from the Scandinavian languages) I usually find myself writing in the Scots segment of my native tongue rather than Glaswegian. 'Yellow on the Broom' is not a translation from another language; it is a song version of Bessie White's prose autobiography. If 'Oor Hamlet' owes something to music-hall, this is informed by my love of traditional songs and especially the other 'broom' refrains: Lay the bent to the bonnie broom; she'll never gang doon to the broom ony mair; the birk and the broom bloom bonnie.

OOR HAMLET

(Air: The Mason's Apron)

There was this king sitting in his gairden a' alane,
When his brither in his ear poured a wee tate o' henbane.
Then he stole his brither's crown an' his money an' his widow.
But the deid king walked an' goat his son an' said, 'Hey, listen, kiddo,
Ah've been kilt an' it's your duty to take revenge on Claudius,
Kill him quick an' clean an' show the nation whit a fraud he is.'
The boay says, 'Right, Ah'll dae it but Ah'll need to play it crafty –
So that naeb'dy will suspect me, Ah'll kid oan that Ah'm a dafty.'

So wi' a' excep' Horatio – an' he trusts him as a friend –
Hamlet, that's the boay, kids oan he's roon' the bend,
An' because he wisnae ready for obligatory killin',
He tried to make the king think he was tuppence aff the shillin'.
Took the mickey oot Polonius, treatit poor Ophelia vile,
Tellt Rosencrantz an' Guildenstern that Denmark was a jile.
Then a troupe o' travellin' actors like 7.84
Arrived to dae a special wan-night gig in Elsinore.

Hamlet! Hamlet! Loved his mammy!
Hamlet! Hamlet! Acting balmy!
Hamlet! Hamlet! Hesitatin',
Wonders if the ghost's a cheat
An' that is how he's waitin'.

Then Hamlet wrote a scene for the players to enact
While Horatio an' him wad watch to see if Claudius cracked.
The play was ca'd 'The Moosetrap' – no the wan that's runnin' noo –
An' sure enough the king walked oot afore the scene was through.
So Hamlet's goat the proof that Claudius gi'ed his da the dose,
The only problem being noo that Claudius knows he knows.
So while Hamlet tells his ma that her new husband's no a fit wan,
Uncle Claud pits oot a contract wi' the English king as hit-man.

Then when Hamlet kilt Polonius, the concealed corpus delecti
Was the king's excuse to send him for an English hempen neck-tie,
Wi' Rosencrantz an' Guildenstern to make sure that he goat there,
But Hamlet jumped the boat an' pit the finger oan that pair.

Meanwhile Laertes heard his da had been stabbed through the arras.
He came racin' back to Elsinore tout suite, hotfoot fae Paris,
An' Ophelia wi' her da kilt by the man she wished to marry –
Eftir sayin' it wi' flooers, she committit hari-kari.

Hamlet! Hamlet! Nae messin'!
Hamlet! Hamlet! Learnt his lesson!
Hamlet! Hamlet! Yorick's crust
Convinced him that men, good or bad,
At last must come to dust.

Then Laertes loast the place an' was demandin' retribution,
An' the king says, 'Keep the heid an' Ah'll provide ye a solution.'
He arranged a sword-fight for the interestit pairties,
Wi' a bluntit sword for Hamlet an' a shairp sword for Laertes.
An' to make things double sure (the auld belt-an'-braces line)
He fixed a poisont sword-tip an' a poisont cup o' wine.
The poisont sword goat Hamlet but Laertes went an' muffed it.
'Cause he goat stabbed hissel, an' he confessed afore he snuffed it.

Hamlet's mammy drank the wine an' as her face turnt blue,
Hamlet says, 'Ah quite believe the king's a baddy noo.'
'Incestuous, treacherous, damned Dane,' he said, to be precise,
An' made up for hesitatin' by killin' Claudius twice.
'Cause he stabbed him wi' the sword an' forced the wine atween his
    lips.
Then he cried, 'The rest is silence!' That was Hamlet hud his chips.
They firet a volley ower him that shook the topmaist rafter,
An' Fortinbras, knee-deep in Danes, lived happy ever after.

Hamlet! Hamlet! A' the gory!
Hamlet! Hamlet! End of story!
Hamlet! Hamlet! Ah'm away!
If you think this is borin'
Ye should read the bloody play!

YELLOW ON THE BROOM

I ken ye dinna like it lass,
To winter here in toon,
For the scaldies aye miscry us
And they try to bring us doon,
And it's hard to raise three bairns
In a single flea-box room,
But I'll tak' ye on the road again
When yellow's on the broom,
    When the yellow's on the broom,
    When the yellow's on the broom,
    I'll tak' ye on the road again
    When yellow's on the broom.

The scaldies ca' us tinker dirt
And sconce oor bairns in school,
But who cares whit a scaldie thinks?
For a scaldie's but a fool.
They never hear the yorlin's sang
Nor see the flax in bloom,
For they're aye cooped up in hooses
When the yellow's on the broom.

Nae sale for pegs nor baskets noo,
So just to stey alive
We've had to work at scaldie jobs
Frae nine o'clock to five,
But we ca' nae man oor maister,
For we own the warld's room,
And we'll bid fareweel to Brechin
When the yellow's on the broom.

I'm weary for the springtime
When we tak' the road aince mair
To the plantin' and the pearlin'
And the berry-fields at Blair,
When we meet up wi' oor kinfolk
Frae a' the country roon',
And the ganaboot folk tak' the road
When yellow's on the broom.

AONGHAS MacNEACAIL

Aonghas MacNeacail, a native Gaelic speaker from Skye, learned English at the age of five, but held on to enough Gaelic to be able to reclaim his own cultural identity by his thirties. For the past decade he has written poetry only in Gaelic; not so much by choice as of psychological and political necessity.

Three poems cannot reveal the full range of a writer's work spanning twenty years or so. Of my selection, one appeared in my first full collection, another in a magazine and the last is too recent to have reached print till now.

They form a kind of triptych, with death as the common thread. The earliest, 'seo agad sinne', represents an attempt to transcend factious politics, fraudulent histories and a harshly redactive religious environment. 'chùm mi seachad' could be a medieval incantation against the Black Death, or some such plague. In our nuclear age it is, sadly, not anachronistic. It is, though, defiantly affirmative, in both movement and *dénouement*. An undertone of political dissent is shared with the first poem and with that on 'marilyn monroe', whose death in no way inhibited those who grasped her commercial potential.

In an increasingly divided society, I am more and more drawn to respond overtly to political questions. At the same time, traditional euphonies become more pronounced in my poetry. I feel that knowledge of the history I spring from has heightened my awareness of the present, while familiarity with *my* portion (the Gaelic lode) of that aspect of history we call 'culture' provides me with the tools to articulate that awareness.

SEO AGAD SINNE

seo agad sinne
'nar seasamh air bile fànais
'n siud   fada bhuainn
a' chruinne bha sinn ri àiteachd

their cuid gur e ifrinn tha romhainn
their cuid gur e pàrras

chan fhaic mise ach
suailean socair a' chadail
àite gun
at, acras no anshocair
gun strì gun shanas cràidh
falamhachd air nach tig atharrachadh
far nach ruig an teanga dhuaireachail
neo-bhith gun deòin no dìoladh
gun eud nimheil a' duaichneachadh
gun fharpais sgàineach airson sgillinn
gun threabhadh raointean uachdarain

chan fhaic, cha chluinn
ach tosd gun chaochladh
tro dhubhar teann sgàile
tha ceileadh oirnn na bile guirm
bile ghorm fànais

HERE WE ARE

here we are
standing on the lip of a void
there   far away
the earth of our husbandry

some say hell confronts us
some say paradise

i see only
the gentle billows of sleep
a place without
bloating, hunger, discomfort
without strife or hint of agony
an unalterable emptiness
beyond reach of the slanderous tongue
non-being without desire or requital
no poisonous jealousy deforming
nor divisive competing for pennies
no ploughing a master's fields

i can see, hear
only stillness unchanging
through a densely-dark veil
which hides from us the blue/green lip
blue/green edge of the void

CHÙM MI SEACHAD

chùm mi seachad air
an tigh far an robh bàs ag àrdan
an tigh far an robh bàs ag àrdan
an tigh far an robh bàs ag àrdan

cha tug mi ainm dha
cha b' aills' e
cha bu chaitheamh

chùm mi seachad

chùm mi seachad air
an t-sràid far an robh bàs a dannsa
an t-sràid far an robh bàs a dannsa
an t-sràid far an robh bàs a dannsa

bha e bocail
bha e sìneadh
bha e sméideadh
fàilte

chùm mi seachad

chùm mi seachad air
a bhaile far an robh bàs air dhaorach
a bhaile far an robh bàs air dhaorach
a bhaile far an robh bàs air dhaorach

cha robh càirdean agam ann
a b' aithne dhomh

chùm mi seachad

bha mi acrach
bha mi aonrach

romham bha an tìr
far an robh bàs na rìgh air,
agus an sluagh anfhoiseil

I KEPT ON PAST

i kept on past
the house where death was rampant
the house where death was rampant
the house where death was rampant

i didn't name it
not cancer it
wasn't consumption

i kept going

i kept on past
the street where death was dancing
the street where death was dancing
the street where death was dancing

it was skipping
it was stretching
it was beckoning
welcome

i kept going

i kept on past
the town where death was drunken
the town where death was drunken
the town where death was drunken

i had no friends there
that i knew of

i kept going

i was hungry
i was alone

ahead was the land
where death was king,
and the folk rebellious

MARILYN MONROE

òr na do ghruaig
òr ann an ìnghnean do chas
òr ann a ruisg cadalach do shùilean beò
òr na do ghruaidhean, nam fathunn athaidh
òr ruadh do bhilean
òr san ghualainn mhìn àrd a fasgadh do smig
òr anns a bhroilleach gealltanach
paisgte na bhad
òr na do chneas sheang, air miadain do chruachan
ann a lùb nan slìasaid is
air glùin nan dìamhaireachd
rinn d'aobroinn òrach
dannsa caol
do gach sùil a shealladh
airgiod beò na do chuislean
airgiod beò na do chridhe
airgiod beò gu na h-iomaill
dhe d'anam
agus d'osnadh, do ghàire
do ghuth-seinn, do ghuth-labhairt
mar bhraoin de dh' òr

agus do gach fear a chum
air lios leaghteach nan dealbh thu
òr, o
bhàrr calgach do chlaiginn gu
buinn rùisgte do chas
òr, òr, òr,
beò no marbh

their cuid nach robh thu cho cùbhraidh
's iad a deoghal an t-sùigh
a sporan suilt òrach do bhian
òr, òr, òr

MARILYN MONROE

gold in your hair
gold in the nails on your feet
gold in the sleepy lids of your living eyes
gold in your cheeks, in their rumour of a blush
red gold of your lips
gold in the raised shoulder that shelters your chin
gold in your breasts, their promise
enfolded in wisps
gold in your slender waist, on the meadows of your hip
in the curve of thigh and
on your knee of mysteries
your golden ankle gave
slim dances
that any eye could see
quicksilver in your veins
quicksilver in your heart
quicksilver to every corner
of your soul
and your sighs, your laugh
your singing, your speech
like a mist of gold

and to every man who kept you
on the screen's dissolving field
gold, from the maned top of your skull
to the bare soles of your feet
gold, gold, gold,
alive or dead

some say you weren't so fragrant
as they suck the substance
from the fertile purse of your skin
gold, gold, gold

ELMA MITCHELL

Born 1919, Airdrie, Lanarkshire. Somerville College, Oxford, 1938–41. Worked in London as librarian in the BBC, publishing, journalism and so on until 1961. Now lives in Somerset. Latest book *People Etcetera* (Peterloo Poets, 1987), containing new poems and selections from earlier volumes, received Scottish Arts Council Spring Book Award 1988.

'This Poem . . .', the most recent of the four, is a light-hearted and ironically stated, but heart-felt introduction to my own and any other poems – intended as a plea to read, live with and enjoy poetry, without worrying about it, nor explaining too much, nor over-examining.

'At First, My Daughter' I chose because it is about happiness (not often celebrated today) and its moment of absolute recognition in a young woman's life, on the birth of her first child. It is not autobiographical.

'Thoughts after Ruskin' was one of my earliest poems to be published (juvenilia excepted), but seems to be still valid and enjoyed. It is not specifically a feminist poem; a woman poet, like any other, must write as she sees, feels and hears.

'The Watch-Dogs' is probably my only 'public' poem, on a theme very pressing in contemporary life. I have tried to use metaphor and irony to convey our ambivalence towards our highly-mechanised defence systems, also potentially destructive of all or any life. So I put it at the end!

THIS POEM . . .

This poem is dangerous: it should not be left
Within the reach of children, or even of adults
Who might swallow it whole, with possibly
Undesirable side-effects. If you come across
An unattended, unidentified poem
In a public place, do not attempt to tackle it
Yourself. Send it (preferably, in a sealed container)
To the nearest centre of learning, where it will be rendered
Harmless, by experts. Even the simplest poem
May destroy your immunity to human emotions.
All poems must carry a Government warning. Words
Can seriously affect your heart.

AT FIRST, MY DAUGHTER

She is world without understanding.
She is made of sound.
She drinks me.

We laugh when I lift her by the feet.
She is new as a petal.
Water comes out of her mouth and her little crotch.

She gives the crook of my arm
A weight of delight.
I stare in her moving mirror of untouched flesh.

Absurd, but verifiable,
These words – mother, daughter –
They taste of receiving and relinquishing.

She will never again be quite so novel and lovely
Nor I so astonished.
In touch, we are celebrating

The first and last moments
Of being together and separate,
Indissolute – till we are split

By time, and growth, and man,
The things I made her with.

THOUGHTS AFTER RUSKIN

Women reminded him of lilies and roses.
Me they remind rather of blood and soap,
Armed with a warm rag, assaulting noses,
Ears, neck, mouth and all the secret places:

Armed with a sharp knife, cutting up liver,
Holding hearts to bleed under a running tap,
Cutting and stuffing, pickling and preserving,
Scalding, blanching, broiling, pulverising,
– All the terrible chemistry of their kitchens.

Their distant husbands lean across mahogany
And delicately manipulate the market,
While safe at home, the tender and the gentle
Are killing tiny mice, dead snap by the neck,
Asphyxiating flies, evicting spiders,
Scrubbing, scouring aloud, disturbing cupboards,
Committing things to dustbins, twisting, wringing,
Wrists red and knuckles white and fingers puckered,
Pulpy, tepid. Steering screaming cleaners
Around the snags of furniture, they straighten
And haul out sheets from under the incontinent
And heavy old, stoop to importunate young,
Tugging, folding, tucking, zipping, buttoning,
Spooning in food, encouraging excretion,
Mopping up vomit, stabbing cloth with needles,
Contorting wool around their knitting needles,
Creating snug and comfy on their needles.

Their huge hands! their everywhere eyes! their voices
Raised to convey across the hullabaloo.
Their massive thighs and breasts dispensing comfort,
Their bloody passages and hairy crannies,
Their wombs that pocket a man upsidedown!

And when all's over, off with overalls
quickly consulting clocks, they go upstairs,
Sit and sigh a little, brushing hair,
And somehow find, in mirrors, colours, odours,
Their essence of lilies and of roses.

THE WATCH-DOGS

Every day, the watch-dogs raise their muzzles
A little higher

They become more sensitive,
Reliable, subtle,
As the century ticks away

The watch-dogs
Do not bear looking at
Nor thinking of
They are susceptible
To tremors and disaffection –
Do not upset them

They can hear grass growing
And the embryo quick in the womb
How long they will tolerate this
We do not know.

WILLIAM MONTGOMERIE

My first poem, 'Glasgow Street', represents the first two decades of my life, at school and university, covering the first section of *From Time to Time* (selected poems set to music by Eddie McGuire), whose central theme was my life, near Parkhead Cross.

My second poem, 'Tay Estuary', I have chosen from my second period on the east coast of Scotland. I married there and we made our home for thirty years in Broughty Ferry, which inspired a number of poems.

The third poem, 'Epitaph' (1941), was written during the Second World War after my younger brother, James, was drowned in his torpedoed ship, off Gibraltar.

My wife and I have gone most summers, to the limits of Europe, east and south. Out of this has come many of our poems.

Thirty years later (1971) we drove by car to the south of Spain and looked across the Straits of Gibraltar to where brother James died. This was the inspiration of my third poem. My fourth poem also has a Spanish theme. Fifty of my poems are still uncollected in print.

Broughty Ferry, during my thirty years there, was a very live centre of folk singing, and I recorded in Angus, Perth and Fife many Scottish folk songs. I have a large collection of folk-rhymes still unpublished. Branching from that, the European Mummers Play, which has branches all over Europe, drew my attention to its influence on Shakespeare, especially on Prince Hamlet's play-within-the-play. A late sixteenth-century picture proves that Hamlet's play is a parody of the Mummers Play, which makes a new interpretation of Hamlet's play necessary, and waiting for a producer. The result is so startling that, apart from a few intellects, this new interpretation is incredible, like many important new discoveries.

GLASGOW STREET

Out of this ugliness may come
Some day, so beautiful a flower
That men will wonder at that hour,
Remembering smoke and flowerless slum.

TAY ESTUARY

The Law
holds in a hollowed hand
hill and river
holds to the far horizon
the sky's blue bubble
turning

Orion turns
and the burning sun
round the Hill
and still Pole
turns on the wheel of the world
turns the shape of the sky

Ships depart
blind lighthouses wait
pilot cutter
and little harbour lights
on a Ness in Angus in the shadow of Fife

Red buoys tilt and turn in the estuary
for ships returning
held by hill and river
ships and sky held by river and hill.

EPITAPH

(for 2nd Officer James S. Montgomerie of the S.S. *Carsbreck*,
torpedoed off Gibraltar, 24 October 1941)

My brother is skull and skeleton now
empty of mind behind the brow
in ribs and pelvis empty space
bone-naked without a face.

On a draughty beach drifting sand
clawed by a dry skeleton hand
sifts in the hourglass of his head
time useless to bones of the dead.

THIRTY YEARS AFTER

(*Tarifa* 1971)

When you woke in the dark
listening from your bunk
to the ship's heartbeat
what fears came to you
from a boy's Glasgow
drowned deep in a man's memory
under curved dolphins
wide-winged gannets
floating isles of blae jellyfish
sea fog
time-fused fears
deeper than nerve-ends of feeling
by day beyond red and violet
by night between dream and dream
between wave-bands of the ship's radio.

Still Hell under the keel
waked to terror
in a U-boat's crab eye
a torpedo between two waves

a bomb from a child's Heaven
Death with a razor in this dark lane
ten miles of rain wide
between our wiped windscreen
here in Spain
and brown beaches and Moroccan white houses in Africa
where nor'-west
Nelson waited for Villeneuve
where *Unterseebooten*
that night waited.

EL CHICO

The navel of your world
Pepe! is not where a paper map of Spain
poises on a pinpoint at Angel's Hill
but in the Meson Canaleja in Jerez here.

This Holy Week beginning
the glass door with typed menus
opens with a draught and soft sift of rain.

Little Pepe!
unnoticed by Americans at the booked table
by wine porters clattering in out in
gulping *aguardiente* on the house
by *Madrileñas* only the head waiter remembers
dusting old memories as tapas to dark brandy.

Behind the tall bar little Pepe with the white apron
you file paper napkins on wire
pack toothpicks in a pewter cup
wipe glasses
tuck the towel in your belt and
keep your place.

Glossary: *Angel's Hill* – south of Madrid, the omphalos of Spain; *aguardiente* –
spirits; *Madrileñas* – natives of Madrid.

EDWIN MORGAN

Born Glasgow 1920. War service with Royal Army Medical Corps, 1940–6. Taught English at University of Glasgow; retired as Titular Professor, 1980. At present Visiting Professor at University of Strathclyde. Books include: *Poems of Thirty Years* (Carcanet, 1982); *Sonnets from Scotland* (Mariscat, 1984); *Selected Poems* (Carcanet, 1985); *Themes on a Variation* (Carcanet, 1988). The poems are chosen from *Poems of Thirty Years*.

The choice is a compromise. The overall length allowed was too short to accommodate some poems I would have wanted to include. However, the two I have chosen can serve as samples. 'Glasgow Green' (1963) is one of many poems I wrote about Glasgow from the later 1950s onwards, and although I might have selected a happier example, like 'Trio', I think the present poem has a deeper meaning for me in that it accepted the challenge, with all its attendant risks, of a difficult subject – urban decay and subterranean sexuality. The dramatised homosexual incident at the core of the poem, violent but in no sense unique, became a springboard into a range of social and spiritual concerns, pleas and prophecies, and so allowed the poem to move through different tones and voices, in a way that I hoped would be felt to be liberating.

Who can say why a memory which has lain hidden in the mind for many years should suddenly force itself on the consciousness and demand to be put into poetry? Nothing seems to be lost. Emotionally charged moments, which at the time were the cause, perhaps, of pain, but not of artistic expression, are like dormant seeds that wait their time, fed invisibly by the mere succession of events. 'The Coals' (1980) embodies a moment of self-recognition, born in the present but conceived in the past.

GLASGOW GREEN

Clammy midnight, moonless mist.
A cigarette glows and fades on a cough.
Meth-men mutter on benches,
pawed by river fog. Monteith Row
sweats coldly, crumbles, dies
slowly. All shadows are alive.
Somewhere a shout's forced out – 'No!' –
it leads to nothing but silence,
except the whisper of the grass
and the other whispers that fill the shadows.

'What d'ye mean see me again?
D'ye think I came here jist for that?
I'm no finished with you yet.
I can get the boys t'ye, they're no that faur away.
You wouldny like that eh? Look there's no two ways aboot it.
Christ but I'm gaun to have you Mac
if it takes all night, turn over you bastard
turn over, I'll . . .'
                    Cut the scene.
Here there's no crying for help,
it must be acted out, again, again.
This is not the delicate nightmare
you carry to the point of fear
and wake from, it is life, the sweat
is real, the wrestling under a bush
is real, the dirty starless river
is the real Clyde, with a dishrag dawn
it rinses the horrors of the night
but cannot make them clean,
though washing blows
                    where the women watch
by day,
        and children run,
                    on Glasgow Green.

And how shall these men live?
Providence, watch them go!
Watch them love, and watch them die!
How shall the race be served?
It shall be served by anguish
as well as by children at play.
It shall be served by loneliness
as well as by family love.
It shall be served by hunter and hunted in their endless chain
as well as by those who turn back the sheets in peace.
The thorn in the flesh!
Providence, water it!
Do you think it is not watered?
Do you think it is not planted?
Do you think there is not a seed of the thorn
as there is also a harvest of the thorn?
Man, take in that harvest!
Help that tree to bear its fruit!
Water the wilderness, walk there, reclaim it!
Reclaim, regain, renew! Fill the barns and the vats!

Longing,
        longing
                shall find its wine.

Let the women sit in the Green
and rock their prams as the sheets
blow and whip in the sunlight.
But the beds of married love
are islands in a sea of desire.
Its waves break here, in this park,
splashing the flesh as it trembles
like driftwood through the dark.

THE COALS

Before my mother's hysterectomy
she cried, and told me she must never bring
coals in from the cellar outside the house,
someone must do it for her. The thing itself
I knew was nothing, it was the thought
of that dependence. Her tears shocked me
like a blow. As once she had been taught,
I was taught self-reliance, discipline,
which is both good and bad. You get things done,
you feel you keep the waste and darkness back
by acts and acts and acts and acts and acts,
bridling if someone tells you this is vain,
learning at last in pain. Hardest of all
is to forgive yourself for things undone,
guilt that can poison life – away with it,
you say, and it is loath to go away.
I learned both love and joy in a hard school
and treasure them like the fierce salvage of
some wreck that has been built to look like stone
and stand, though it did not, a thousand years.

TOM POW

Born in Edinburgh 1950. Studied St Andrews and Aberdeen. *Rough Seas* (Canongate, 1987), Scottish Arts Council Book Award. *In Verse* (Scottish Television). Interviewed nine major Scottish poets 1987–8. *The Execution of Mary Timney* (Radio Play – BBC Radio Scotland). Broadcast November 1988. Guest of Soviet Writers' Union, October 1988. Major Scottish Arts Council Writer's Bursary 1988–9. Teacher of English at Dumfries Academy.

I find myself agreeing more and more with the American naturalist Annie Dillard that 'Seeing is the pearl of great price' – and the poets I warm to most, such as MacCaig, Heaney and Elizabeth Bishop, are the ones who can make us see. I hope that these three poems show a delight in seeing; that the eye and ear have worked well together to capture the physical environment of the poems – be that the jittery *edge* of the Bronx, my sister's back garden or the beautiful Galloway landscape.

I know you shouldn't let critics tell you what you are about, but when, in a review of my book *Rough Seas*, James Aitchison wrote that my 'underlying purpose is to recreate an experience in order to discover its true nature', it struck me as being a very perceptive comment; and one which I think these three poems uphold, concerned as they are with the experiences of love and fear, the resonances of childhood and the sheer elation I've found 'Summer Running' in Galloway.

Yes, it matters to me very much that the poem feels true. However, I think this can still be the case, even if, as I have found myself doing recently, I am recreating an experience from deep in the past that may never have happened at all.

LOVE AT THE (BRONX) ZOO

We walk the icy paths
past frozen ponds, snowed-in enclosures,
where reeds like drifting porcupine
and black huts are all that show.

In the dim warmth of an animal house,
we linger by a tank
with a sandy-coloured,
soft-shelled turtle, the size
of my spread hand. From the long spoon
of its head, nostrils stick out
like tiny binoculars. Eyes,
two silvery stains. When it rises
from the dark green weed, its fins,
like sycamore seeds, brush the window
we peer through. So close is it
and so angled, we see

the thin loop of its down-turned mouth;
almost fancy it would speak . . .

Back in the Bronx, we don't know
which blind-eyed alley to turn down;
eventually are wrong anyway. We ride around –
a fly caught in deadly nightshade – trying
to reclaim the rim of the highway

past burned-out buildings, waste-ground;
a brazier licking the chill
off some winos.

A battered blue cadillac jerks
to a stop in front of us. Rusted panels
shake; red tail lights glare
from corroded fins. We sit tight
as the black man's black curses plume

into the winter air. We turn to each other –
sudden neophytes, who might – sleepless, speechless,
in the dark cage of night – hold their soft bodies
close; fear
for love's survival.

THE MOTH-TRAP

In the centre of the sloping lawn, light
from a moth-trap floods the garden – surreal
as if thought walked a green ceiling and sight
in such strangeness became a matter of feel.

The cut-out trees, the black teeth of a fence
mark the limits of this ordered landscape;
gleaming on the horizon its last defence –
the even lights of a runway roped

across the night. Two fat poplar hawks thud
dully against glass along with a smirr
of lesser life: creatures not of blood
or substance, their death – a silvery smeer.

A meagre haul this, till two boys tilt
into light, to match elastic shadows
and faces white as saucers of milk.
Each new element they dive in draws

a measure of proof. And so we observe
one the light calms, the other light excites;
one's a campfire Indian, the other's nerves
are taut, conscious of the wider night.

The light gives his naked movements the grace
of a wild boy reared on the forest floor.
Clothing them with laughter, he lifts his face –
there is nothing yet that can't be shared.

'Isn't childhood . . .?' But I have answered yes
before you finish, still feeling the impress
of something wounded but wonderful
beating inside me against the darkness.

SUMMER RUNNING

The chestnut that all winter
cast broken rods on the water
now dips a head, full as a bison's,
to drink.

The once bald arterial oak
crowns the field like a green
rococo keep.

And our quiddity? Our glory?

We arrive – new-born –
beneath the green light of birch arrows,
hoping, if we run hard enough,
to live in a season, where the tang of wild garlic
is the only hint of loss

and the haze of bluebells is everywhere,
like desire.

TESSA RANSFORD

Director of the Scottish Poetry Library and founder/organiser of the School of Poets (1981), Tessa was born in India, educated in Scotland. Later she lived and worked in Pakistan for eight years. She has published six volumes of poetry of which the latest is *A Dancing Innocence*, Macdonald, Edinburgh. She has read her work recently in Canada and Germany as well as in Scotland.

'Voice in the Night'. This was inspired by Blues singing and rhythms. The search for meaning, faith in the dignity of human life despite suffering and degradation, the transformative properties of art are all represented for me in the Blues.

'Nocturne (Lewis)'. A rhythmical lyric bringing into play many of my favourite themes: the darkness that enhances our light, sorrow that sharpens our joy, the temporary in its context within the permanent, whether in rocks, human settlements, transcendant illumination in wisdom and love.

'Girl Raking Hay: 1918'. A short poem using a tight form and strict rhyme scheme, broadened to assonance. Inspired by a photograph of my mother it tries to express the enormity of what the young suffered in the First World War.

'Indian Women at Windermere'. Perhaps this brings together my own Indian and British selves in any attempt to 'walk tall' as a woman, without avoiding burdens and responsibilities.

VOICE IN THE NIGHT

If passion slows to tempo of a blues
lament and pain sharpens the shoulder blade
and still my arm goes down to fingertips
and friendly voice is gravelly with death
residing in the throat, so that the song
itself of life is blistered through with note
of its mortality and mine, which might
be sooner than my mother's in her failing
wits, and leave my lover lonely, who
has given me a taste of what it is
to lose, the more to find, my singing soul.

I'll lie no longer in the dark, but rise,
put on the light, consult whatever serves
as oracle, without a pilgrimage
save that of Lao Tsu or Socrates
or Christ and those interpreters of theirs,
who may have heard the crazy voices that
directed them to seek an early death
for an imaginative cause that made
the world too good to leave unsacrificed.

I'll tell my children not to suffer fools
nor think themselves unwise in judging from
experience, and living at the highest
point of contradiction, where
music breaks from human bitterness
and simple gestures of the mind or mood
transcend such limits as engender them.

NOCTURNE (LEWIS)

It is raining on Lewis in the night
Darkness has brimmed over the hills
spilling upon the moor
and dropping into circles of inland sea.

Last night the moon was wildly shed
by mountain and cloud to reveal a sheer
countenance at the window
and blending with the water in bright festoons;

But tonight the dark is raining on Lewis:
on the black-house with its hunched thatch
on battered, abandoned buses
derelict cars and stacks of murky peat.

Boats are plying under the rain
and enormous eels under the boats
and fishing nets are lifted
up and under the tide like diving birds.

For thousands of years of nights the stones
have loomed in lonely communion
beneath the moon, the rain,
ritually aloof, cleansed and illumined.

And the white schist of my lasting self
safe and awake yet exposed to love –
its darkness and shafts of light –
takes up position in line with primeval wisdom.

GIRL RAKING HAY: 1918

She laughs in the hayfield, sixteen, slight,
over her shoulder a chestnut plait,
broad-brimmed hat
and long skirt,
summer, hay day, August heat,
1918, peace not yet.

The huge hayrake is twice her size,
her hands that wield it, like lilies;
death the news,
her brother dies.
While girls all yearn for armistice
the hay falls scythed about their knees.

INDIAN WOMEN AT WINDERMERE

Indian women at Windermere
why carry plastic buckets and pans
stooped and bending low,
when you know
how to sail along like swans
your loads aloft as head-gear?

Oldish women in walking-shoes,
saris, coats and spectacles,
with wealthy, westernised sons
Indians
living in modern bungalows –
how much of yourselves have you had to lose?

If I were you I would wish to be
inconspicuous yet walking tall;
no slavery
to nationality
whether in Britain or Bengal –
head high and both hands free.

ALASTAIR REID

I began writing poems in Scotland, and have continued to do so, spasmodically, all over the place. I have spent about a third of my life in Scotland, and the rest in Spain, the United States and Latin America, writing a great variety of things. I live now in the Caribbean, on a far peninsula in the Dominican Republic, growing ginger; and I expect to go on writing, poems and prose, until the pencil falls from my lifeless fingers.

Once written and published, poems follow quite different careers. Some remain private, and stay close to home, like family ghosts, while others go public and have separate careers, finding their way into odd places – anthologies, other languages, bathroom mirrors, examination papers, other people's memories. I have chosen three such public poems.

The first, 'Scotland', was a given poem, in that it happened to me, in the wake of a spring walk in St Andrews. I think of it less as a poem of mine than as a small chronicle of our contradictions, for the record.

'My Father, Dying', which I wrote as a precise and private account of a month in the Borders, as my father was dying, has served, I have been told a number of times, as a kind of talisman for others facing a similar experience; and 'A Lesson in Music', about entering music, beyond the limits of language, has appealed to a lot of musicians – one violinist I know keeps it in the lid of his fiddle case.

Uselessness, we have been told, is one of the qualities of pure art; but the notion that some poems may prove useful is one that appeals to me. I look on poems much as I look on recipes: they do not do the cooking for you, but they help.

SCOTLAND

It was a day peculiar to this piece of the planet,
when larks rose on long thin strings of singing
and the air shifted with the shimmer of actual angels.
Greenness entered the body. The grasses
shivered with presences, and sunlight
stayed like a halo on hair and heather and hills.
Walking into town, I saw, in a radiant raincoat,
the woman from the fish-shop. 'What a day it is!'
cried I, like a sunstruck madman.
And what did she have to say for it?
Her brow grew bleak, her ancestors raged in their graves
as she spoke with their ancient misery:
'We'll pay for it, we'll pay for it, we'll pay for it!'

MY FATHER, DYING

At summer's succulent end,
the house is green-stained.
I reach for my father's hand

and study his ancient nails.
Feeble-bodied, yet at intervals
a sweetness appears and prevails.

The heavy-scented night
seems to get at his throat.
It is as if the dark coughed.

In the other rooms of the house,
the furniture stands mumchance.
Age has engraved his face.

Cradling his wagged-out chin,
I shave him, feeling bone
stretching the waxed skin.

By his bed, the newspaper lies furled.
He has grown too old
to unfold the world,

which has dwindled to the size of a sheet.
His room has a stillness to it.
I do not call it waiting, but I wait,

anxious in the dark, to see if
the butterfly of his breath
has fluttered clear of death.

There is so much might be said,
dear old man, before I find you dead;
but we have become too separate

now in human time
to unravel all the interim
as your memory goes numb.

But there is no need for you to tell –
no words, no wise counsel,
no talk of dying well.

We have become mostly hands
and voices in your understanding.
The whole household is pending.

I am not ready
to be without your frail and wasted body,
your miscellaneous mind-way,

the faltering vein of your life.
Each evening, I am loth
to leave you to your death.

Nor will I dwell on
the endless, cumulative question
I ask, being your son.

But on any one
of these nights soon,
for you, the dark will not crack with dawn,

and then I will begin
with you that hesitant conversation
going on and on and on.

A LESSON IN MUSIC

Play the tune again: but this time
with more regard for the movement at the source of it
and less attention to time. Time falls
curiously in the course of it.

Play the tune again: not watching
your fingering, but forgetting, letting flow
the sound till it surrounds you. Do not count
or even think. Let go.

Play the tune again: but try to be
nobody, nothing, as though the pace
of the sound were your heart beating, as though
the music were your face.

Play the tune again. It should be easier
to think less every time of the notes, of the measure.
It is all an arrangement of silence. Be silent, and then
play it for your pleasure.

Play the tune again; and this time, when it ends,
do not ask me what I think. Feel what is happening
strangely in the room as the sound glooms over
you, me, everything.

Now,
play the tune again.

STEPHEN SCOBIE

I was born in Scotland, and spent the first twenty-one years of my life there, but I have now lived longer in Canada than I did in Scotland.

The poem I have chosen for this anthology is the first section of a longer poem, called 'Dunino', which will be published by Véhicule Press in Montreal, Canada. The poem thus reflects my double allegiance to Scotland and to Canada.

In 'Dunino', the interchange between Scotland and Canada, between past and present, is triangulated through a third point, an Other, an intermediary, which in this case is Germany. The opening of the poem is set in Grainau (a village in the Bavarian Alps, at the foot of the Zugspitze), which I was visiting, in February 1985, to attend a conference on Canadian literature. While this provides a Canadian connection for the German references, the Scottish link is derived from the similarity between the name Duino, the site of Rilke's great Elegies, and Dunino, a small farming community in East Fife, near St Andrews, where I went to university. The Rilke poem provides the 'other', the intermediary of desire, for both Canada and Scotland. Short quotations from 'The Duino Elegies' appear in my text translated into Scots: for Canadian readers, this will be almost as 'foreign' as the original German; and even Scottish readers should not find it completely familiar, since I use a 'synthetic' Scots, *à la* MacDiarmid, not the authentic dialect of any one region. The various interplays of Scotland, Canada and Germany set up a shifting structure of references within which, I hope, the poem can develop the more personal tune of elegy: for my father, for my own childhood, for the country in which I was born and which I have never really left.

DUNINO

An gin I were tae girn aa nicht
wha, amang the angels o the lift,
wad bend a lug?

– the Silence!
It was like: no, it was not 'like'
anything. It was Grainau, Badersee,
the German woods; it was February,
early morning, the snow came sifting,
tree-gentled, onto the lake. I was
first on the path, and alone, with the
creaking of my footsteps as they fell,
inscribing their slowly erasing trace,
a circuit of the Badersee. Mist rose
from its hot-spring waters: the paddle
of ducks, their occasional cry, and my
shoes' creaking, these were the only sounds
and I stopped, often, to hear the silence
there in the woods of Grainau, under the hidden sign
of the mountain, Zugspitze, shrouded out
in the snow that fell like: no, not 'like'
anything. In the snow that fell.

This was beauty, but not terror.
This was beauty one could feel at home in,
welcome, to loveliest earth.

It dwines, it slides, it slips away
in a moment's movement: finger on shutter,
the camera clicks its fractioned second
and you are left, months afterward,
a thin and paper image, the falling
snow as a blur on the lens, white magic,
a sign of what you can only breathe
in awe: the Silence! and the woods are gone.
For *ilka angel gars us greet*
with dread, with joy, with the pain of earth
as it waits for our hamewith turning.

> *An aye we lo'e it aa the mair*
> *because it winna fash its heid*
> *wi the bother o dingan us doon –*

for always there is home and home:
the place we return to, relieved, and then

the place we know, we have never been.

Nicht, mirk nicht, whan aa thae snell
'wunds wi warlds tae swing'
blaw intae oor een . . .

Desire never so distant
as when we walk the familiar ways:
horizon slipping over edge of earth.
So Konrad spoke of the town he was born
beyond the border in East Germany
accepting without rancour the divide
he could not cross: driving from Lübeck to Kiel
through Schleswig's February landscape grey,
does it not, he asked me, remind you of
Scotland? – for always there is home
and always returning: overnight
by sleeper from London, lying
horizontal across the rails, and waking
early, to open the blind
on a Scottish tree

– some birk on the braeside there
ye maun pass i the mornin-blink –

a first arrival, to translate me from
'the seas o the high Germanie' –

'And there's the end o ane auld sang':
Lord Chancellor Seafield, legendarily
turning his face to the wall, the song
echoing ever since. On the sea. In the fields.

Fife, East Fife, the harvest stooking
gowd of grain in the rolling fields,
the hedgerows' scattered punctuation
under the height of Kellie Law;
East Neuk of Fife, the fishers' margin,
driftnet of villages pursing the shore,
the boats that fix their silver meads
over the kirk to Kellie Law.

And here the poem declared its title
before a line had yet been written:
it was a roadsign, the name of a village
– Dunino – where no village is.
A scatter of farms, a school, and one
red telephone box: but even that
a mile down the road. From the sign
there is nothing in sight. 'Dunino' –
and then the harvest fields.
Not a place I've ever stopped, although
for years of my life I used to drive through
on the road from St Andrews south,
the Anstruther road, up over the hill, turn
west at Drumrack farm, and home
to Carnbee. Facing out to the Forth:
my father's parish. My father's grave.

> *It is an unco orra thing*
> *tae be nae langer o the yird,*
> *tae gang nae mair the scarce-kent ways*
> *nor seek the dern sense o the burnan rose.*
> *It is an unco orra thing*
> *tae set aside yir vera name,*
> *tae lang nae mair til langin's limit*
> *but watch yir hert's benmaist desires*
> *bauchle awa like a rag on the rain.*

The dead, says Rilke, are never gone
and even the angels who move among us
cannot distinguish which we are.
In the wood of the Lorimer carving
on the pulpit of Carnbee church
(the bell-rope swings behind the window),
a pelican lances her own bright breast,
and blood is written on the leesome white.

– the Silence! and the woods are gone.

ALEXANDER SCOTT

An Aberdonian, Scott spent his professional life as a university teacher, mainly in Glasgow. He has produced seven collections of poems in English and Scots, critical studies, plays in verse and in prose, short stories and a biography, and has edited magazines, anthologies, and selections of prose and poetry.

Since the compiler of this book has attacked me elsewhere for an alleged inability to choose good poems for anthologisation, I have relied here on other editors, limiting the required selection of some eighty-five lines from my work to examples of those of my poems that have been republished fifteen times or more.

'Calvinist Sang' (1945) is only the third of my post-MacDiarmid poems in Scots to be written, and the first to be anthologised. It is included here as one of the earliest, and not the least effective, of my satirical lyrics.

'Continent o Venus' (1948) is not only the first of my love-poems in Scots but also the most passionate and most paradoxical.

From twenty years later, 'Ballade of Beauties' is among the most widely published of my poems in English. Its direct assault on the emotions of anger, grief and love is made bearable only by the strict control of its form. The two epigrams, from the often-anthologised sequence, 'Scotched', are among my more comic cuts, while 'Problems' (1972), with its Scots expression of the international themes of space exploration and imperialistic war, has had a corresponding international success, achieving publication in Europe and the States as well as Scotland. The critical acclaim which this poem has received suggests that it is one of my more powerful works in free verse.

CALVINIST SANG

A hunder pipers canna blaw
　　Our trauchled times awa,
Drams canna droun them out, nor sang
Hap their scarecraw heids for lang.

Gin aa the warld was bleezan fou,
　　What gowk wad steer the plou?
Gin chiels were cowpan quines aa day.
They'd mak (but fail to gaither) hay.

Pit by your bagpipes, brak your gless,
　　Wi quines, keep aff the gress,
The-day ye need a hert and harns
As dour as the diamant, cauld as the starns.

CONTINENT O VENUS

She lies ablow my body's lust and love,
A country dearly-kent, and yet sae fremd
That she's at aince thon Tir-nan-Og I've dreamed,
The airt I've lived in, whaur I mean to live,
And mair, much mair, a mixter-maxter warld
Whaur fact and dream are taigled up and snorled.

I ken ilk bay o aa her body's strand,
Yet ken them new ilk time I come to shore,
For she's the uncharted sea whaur I maun fare
To find anither undiscovered land,
To find it fremd, and yet to find it dear,
To seek it aye, and aye be bydan there.

BALLADE OF BEAUTIES

Miss Israel Nineteen-Sixty-Eight is new,
A fresh-poured form her swimsuit moulds to sleekness,
Legs long, breasts high, the shoulders firm and true,
The waist a lily wand without a weakness,
The hair, *en brosse* and black, is shorn to bleakness,
Yet shines as stars can make the midnight do –
But still my mind recalls more maiden meekness,
Miss Warsaw Ghetto Nineteen-Forty-Two.

Her masters filmed her kneeling stripped to sue
The mercy barred as mere unmanning weakness,
Or raking rubbish-dumps for crusts to chew,
Or licking boots to prove her slavish meekness,
Or baring loins to lie beneath the bleakness
Of conquerors' lust (and forced to smile it through),
Her starving flesh a spoil preferred to sleekness,
Miss Warsaw Ghetto Nineteen-Forty-Two.

The prize she won was given not to few
But countless thousands, paid the price of meekness,
And paid in full, with far too high a due,
By sadist dreams transformed to functioned sleekness,
A pervert prophet's weakling hate of weakness
Constructing a mad machine that seized and slew,
The grave her last reward, the final bleakness,
Miss Warsaw Ghetto Nineteen-Forty-Two.

Princesses, pale in death or sunned in sleekness,
I dedicate these loving lines to you,
Miss Israel Sixty-Eight and (murdered meekness)
Miss Warsaw Ghetto Nineteen-Forty-Two.

SCOTCH EDUCATION
I tellt ye
I tellt ye.

SCOTCH PASSION
Forgot
Mysel.

PROBLEMS
('We've got a problem here.' – *Apollo 13* report on oxygen-tank failure).

The haill warld waited,
ten hunder million herts
in as monie mouths,
the haill warld harkened
til quaet voices
briggan the black howes o space
wi licht hope
o shipwrack saved,
the mune's mariners
steered through the stark lift
on a lifeline o skeelie science
(the wyve o human harns,
a hunder thousan hankan thegither
owre aa the waft o the warld)
that haled them frae toom heaven
to hame i the sea's haven
– and aye wi the camera's ee
the michty millions watched.

Ahint our backs,
the brukken corps o coolies
cam sooman alang the sworl
o the mirk Mekong,
their wyve o human harns
warped by the skeelie science
that made the machinegun's mant
the proof o pouer
to connach lifelines.

We hae a problem here.

TOM SCOTT

Tom Scott, born 1918 in Glasgow, taken to St Andrews in 1931 because of the slump in the shipyards where his father was a boiler-maker. His father, aged forty-four, went to work with his grandfather, F D Baillie the builder, as a labourer, gradually picking up the mason trade as he went. A sair darg for an ex-foreman boiler-maker. Tom went to Madras College for a year and a half, leaving in 1933 to start earning, first as butcher's message boy, later in the building trade. He served during the Second World War, two years in Nigeria, then London where he stayed till 1953 when he went to Newbattle Abbey College under Edwin Muir and settled in Edinburgh, taking an MA and PhD at Edinburgh University in English and Scots Literature and Language. This poem was written in London in 1951, and was a turning-point in his life. He had just returned from Sicily where he had spent a few months on a Rockefeller Trust Atlantic Award – another turning-point in his life. In Sicily he discovered the Greek world, and out of the shadow of London, wrote a poem about Telemachos which began to fill up with Scots, leading to 'Brand the Builder' and the rest of his work in Scots.

Questions of space made this the only possible choice from my shorter poems. It is drawn from a pre-1939 St Andrews (Sant Aundraes, to the locals) working-class life, and the trade of stonemason, now all but extinct. One must imagine the silence in a near carless era, unpolluted air.

BRAND THE BUILDER

(St Andrews)

On winter days, aboot the gloamin oor
Whan the nock on the college touer
Is chappan lowsin-time
And ilka mason packs his mell and tools awa
Ablow his banker, and bien forenenst the waa
The labourer haps the lave o the lime
Wi soppan secks, to keep it frae a frost, or faa
o suddent snaw
Duran the nicht,
And scrawnie craws flap in the shell-green licht
Towards yon bane-bare rickle o trees
That heeze
Up on the howe abuin the toun,
And the red goun
Is happan mony a student frae the snell nor-easter,
Malcolm Brand, the maister,
Seean the last hand throu the yett
Afore he bars and padlocks it,
Taks ae look roond his stourie yaird
Whaur chunks o stane are liggan
Like the ruins o some auld-farrant biggin:
Picks a skelf oot o his baerd,
Scliffs his tacketty buits, and syne
Clunters hamelins doun the wyn'.

Alang the shore
The greinan white sea-stallions champ and snore.

The main street echoes back his clinkan fuit-faas
Frae its waas
Whaur owre the kerb and causeys yallow licht
Presses back the mirk nicht
As shop-fronts flüde the pavin-stanes in places,
Like the peintit faces
Whures pit on, or actresses – ay, or meenisters –
To plaese their different customers.

But aye the nordren nicht, cauld as rumour,
Taks command,
Chills the haill toun wi his militarie humour
And plots his map o starns wi daedly hand.

Doun by the sea
Murns the white swaw owre the wrack ayebydanlie.

Stoupan throu the anvil pend
Gaes Brand,
And owre the coort wi the twa-three partan creels,
The birss air fu
o the smell o the sea, and fish, and meltit glue,
Draws up at his door, and syne
Hawkan his craig afore he gangs in ben,
Gies a bit scrape at the grater wi his heels.

The kail-pat on the hob is hotteran fu
o the uisual hash o Irish stew,
And by the grate, a red-haired bewtie frettit thin,
His wife is kaain a spurtle roond.
He swaps his buits for his baffies, but a soond.
The twa-three bairns ken to mak nae din
When faither's in,
And sit on creepies roond aboot.
Brand gies a muckle yawn, and howks his paper oot.

Tither side the fire
The kettle hums like a telephone wire.

    'Lord, for what we are about to receive
    Help us to be truly thankful. Aimen.
    Wumman, ye've pit ingans in't again!'

    'Gae wa, ye coorse auld hypocrite!
    Thank the Lord for yir maet, syne grue at it!'

Wi chowks drawn ticht in a speakless scunner
He glowers on her:
Syne on the quaet and straucht-faced bairns:
Faulds his paper doun by his eatin-airns
And, ti the tick-tockan o the nock
Sups, and reads, wi nae ither word nor look.

The warld ootside
Like a lug-held seashell roars wi the rinnan tide.

The denner owre, Brand redds up for the nicht.
Aiblins there's a schedule for to price
Or somethin nice
On at the picters – sacont hoose –
Or some poleetical meetin wants his licht,
Or aiblins, wi him t-total aa his life,
No able to seek the pub to flee the wife,
Daunders oot the West Sands 'on the loose'.
Whatever tis,
The waater slorps frae his elbucks as he synds his phiz.

And this is aa the life he kens there is?

IAIN CRICHTON SMITH

Born 1928 on the Island of Lewis. Went to Aberdeen University where I took an MA Honours in English and where I met many potential poets. Spent twenty-five years teaching English, mostly in Oban High School. I am bilingual, speaking and writing in both English and Gaelic. I have written novels, poems, plays, short stories, criticism, in both languages. My most recent books are *In the Middle of the Wood* (novel), published by Gollancz, and *A Life* (poems) published by Carcanet. All the chosen poems are taken from *Selected Poems* (1985), published by Carcanet.

'Old Woman'. This poem arose from a real incident in the Island of Lewis. The image of the seaweed came when I went down to the shore after I had seen the old woman in her bed.

'Two Girls Singing'. I was travelling on a bus to Dumbarton from Oban. It was a dull dark night in winter. Some people had been sick. Then the girls began to sing quite spontaneously and the whole atmosphere changed as if winter had turned to summer.

'Jean Brodie's Children' was written after I read the book by Muriel Spark. It arose from my fascination at the contrast between children and teachers. Children have their lives before them, teachers not.

'In the Chinese Restaurant'. This is a strange poem whose origin I do not understand. It is a kind of surreal 'John Anderson my Jo'. The Chinese restaurant becomes a kind of paradise and the power of love is imagined by the fact they can suddenly understand Chinese.

'The Exiles'. This was written after I visited Canada and saw the evidence of exile from the Highlands. The imagery in the poem refers to the exile-ships, especially sailing ships.

'You are at the Bottom of my Mind'. This is a love poem translated from the Gaelic. In purely Freudian terms the bottom of the sea is compared to the subconscious. At one time too I was fascinated by Freud. The subconscious remains whether we like it or not.

OLD WOMAN

And she, being old, fed from a mashed plate
as an old mare might droop across a fence
to the dull pastures of its ignorance.
Her husband held her upright while he prayed

to God who is all-forgiving to send down
some angel somewhere who might and perhaps
in his foreign wings among the gradual crops.
She munched, half dead, blindly searching the spoon.

Outside, the grass was raging. There I sat
imprisoned in my pity and my shame
that men and women having suffered time
should sit in such a place, in such a state,

and wished to be away, yes, to be far away
with athletes, heroes, Greeks or Roman men
who pushed their bitter spears into a vein
and would not spend an hour with such decay.

'Pray, God,' he said, 'We ask you, God,' he said.
The bowed back was quiet. I saw the teeth
tighten their grip around a delicate death.
And nothing moved within the knotted head

but only a few poor veins as one might see
vague wishless seaweed floating on a tide
of all the salty waters where had died
too many waves to mark two more or three.

TWO GIRLS SINGING

It neither was the words nor yet the tune
Any tune would have done and any words.
Any listener or no listener at all.

As nightingales in rocks or a child crooning
in its own world of strange awakening
or larks for no reason but themselves.

So on the bus through late November running
by yellow lights tormented, darkness falling,
the two girls sang for miles and miles together

and it wasn't the words or tune, it was the singing.
It was the human sweetness in that yellow,
the unpredicted voices of our kind.

JEAN BRODIE'S CHILDREN

Jean Brodie's children in your small green caps,
I hear you twitter down the avenues.

The great round bell rings out, the Mademoiselle
despairs of English. In the rustling dorms
you giggle under sheets.

'Dear Edinburgh, how I remember you,
your winter cakes and tea, your bright red fire,
your swirling cloaks and clouds.

Your grammar and your Greek, the hush of leaves,
No Orchids for Miss Blandish with a torch
beneath the tweedy blanket.

Ah, those beautiful days, all green and shady,
our black and pleated skirts, our woollen stockings,
our ties of a calm mauve.

Mistresses, iron in their certainty,
their language unambiguous, but their lives
trembling on grey boughs.'

IN THE CHINESE RESTAURANT

Because we'd never go there, it was good,
those years together. We'd never need to go

though we could talk of it, and so we were

happy together in a place we'd made

so small and airless that we couldn't leave.
But we could think of it and say, 'Perhaps

we'll go there someday.' But we could not go

for as we lived so we'd lost all the maps.
It grew more perfect as the slow years passed
as if we were there already. One fine day

we'd find it all around us if we looked.
We would be in it, even old and grey.

So that, one night, in that late restaurant,
with Chinese waiters round us, we picked up
the menu in Chinese and understood

every single word of it. It was
a revelation when the waiters smiled.

They looked so clear as the glasses slowly filled.

NA H-EIL THIRICH

A liuthad soitheach a dh'fhàg ar duthaich
le sgiathan geala a' toirt Chanada orra.
Tha iad mar neapaigearan 'nar ciumhne
's an sàl mar dheòirean
's anns na croinn aca sèoladairean a' seinn
mar eoin air gheugan.

Muir a' Mhàigh ud gu gorm a' ruith,
gealach air an oidhch', grian air an latha,
ach a' ghealach mar mheas buidhe
mar thruinnsear air balla,
ris an tog iad an làmhan
neo mar mhagnet airgeadach
le gathan goirte
a' sruthadh don chridhe.

THE EXILES

The many ships that left our country
with white wings for Canada.
They are like handkerchiefs in our memories
and the brine like tears
and in their masts sailors singing
like birds on branches.

That sea of May running in such blue,
a moon at night, a sun at daytime,
and the moon like a yellow fruit
like a plate on a wall,
to which they raise their hands
like a silver magnet
with piercing rays
streaming into the heart.

THA THU AIR AIGEANN M'INTINN

Gun fhios dhomh tha thu air aigeann m'inntinn
mar fhear-tadhail grunnd na mara
le chlogaid's a dhà shùil mhóir
's chan aithne dhomh ceart d'fhiamh neo do dhòigh
an déidh cóig bliadhna shiantan
tìme dòrtadh eadar mise 's tu:

beanntan bùirn gun ainm a' dòrtadh
eadar mise gad shlaodadh air bòrd
's d'fhiamh 's do dhòighean 'nam 'làmhan fann.
Chaidh thu air chall
am measg lusan dìomhair a' ghrunna
anns an leth-sholus uaine gun ghradh,

's chan éirich thu chaoidh air bhàrr cuain
a chaoidh's mo làmhan a' slaodadh gun sgur
's chan aithne dhomh do shlighe idir
thus' ann an leth-sholus do shuain
a'mtathaich aigeann na mara gun tàmh
's mise slaodadh's a' slaodadh air uachdar caain.

YOU ARE AT THE BOTTOM OF MY MIND

Without my knowing it, you are at the bottom of my mind, like one who visits the bottom of the sea with his helmet and his two great eyes: and I do not know properly your expression or your manner after five years of the showers of time pouring between you and me,

Nameless mountains of water pouring between me, hauling you on board, and your expression and manners in my weak hands. You went astray among the mysterious foliage of the sea-bottom in the green half-light without love.

And you will never rise to the surface of the sea, even though my hands should be ceaselessly hauling, and I do not know your way at all, you in the half-light of your sleep, haunting the bottom of the sea without ceasing, and I hauling and hauling on the surface of the ocean.

ALAN SPENCE

Alan Spence was born in Glasgow in 1947, has travelled a bit and now lives in Edinburgh where he and his wife run the Sri Chinmoy Meditation Centre. Books include *Its Colours they are Fine* (short stories), *Sailmaker* and *Space Invaders* (plays), *Glasgow Zen* and *Ah!* (poetry). A novel, *The Magic Flute*, is due for publication soon.

The sonnet, 'Desire and Time', was written fairly recently, and was my first attempt at the strict sonnet form. It's a form that seems to lend itself to the articulation of the kind of realisation this poem is dealing with – the perception of a truth, unfolding, coming clear.

The 'Four Haiku' show another kind of direct perception, into 'the life of things', the moment illumined. I've been writing haiku for twenty years, and the problem was which four to select out of over a hundred. In the end, I just chose the four that came to mind when I sat down to type them. Seems fair enough!

'Glasgow Zen' also insisted on being included. Glasgow terseness and reductionism at work in areas of philosophical speculation.

'Song' wrote itself one fine clear evening at Glencoe. I was travelling with some friends and we had stopped for a silent meditation out in the open air. Somewhere a bird was singing, and it sang this song into my clear empty receptive mind. It came unbidden and complete, and its nursery rhyme quality was like nothing I'd ever written before. It's a matter of some pride that a school in the East End of Glasgow has adopted it as their school song (sung to the tune of 'The Red Flag').

SONNET: DESIRE AND TIME

I know desire is time, time is desire
but still I cannot raise myself above
desire and time; they burn me in their fire
and keep me from eternity and love.
Yet I have known desirelessness, have flown,
timeless, eternal, free in love's clear sky.
I fall back. Time has cut me to the bone.
I fall. Desire has sucked the marrow dry.
Yet something deep remembers, still would soar
across that sky of unhorizoned joy.
I burn and am consumed, all but this core
that fire cannot burn, cannot destroy.
Desiring, I possess and am possessed,
timebound. In love I live forever blessed.

FOUR HAIKU

the spring breeze –
the paper flowers also
tremble

the moon moves with us
as we walk,
drifts from tree to tree

the whole sky and more
reflected in each raindrop
hanging from that branch

mouse-tracks
across the frozen lard
in the frying pan.

GLASGOW ZEN

On the oneness of self and universe
                 IT'S AW WAN
                 TAE ME

On the ultimate identity of matter and spirit, form and void
                 WHAT'S THE MATTER?
                 NUTHIN!

On the suchness of things
                       AYE, THIS IS IT.
                       THIS IS THE THING

On identity in difference
                 SIX AN
                 HAUF A DOZEN

On the implicit dualism of value judgements
                 IT'S AWFUL
                 GOOD

SONG

the littlest bird
sang all for me
its song was love
it set me free

sang at my birth
and at my death
it sang its song
with my last breath

the littlest bird
sang in my soul
its song was joy
it made me whole

it made me whole
it set me free
it sang its song
its song was me

DERICK THOMSON

Born 1921, Stornoway, Isle of Lewis. Educated Nicolson Institute,
Aberdeen and Cambridge among other places. Professor of Celtic,
University of Glasgow since 1963. Married Carol Galbraith.
Founder and Editor of *Gairm* since 1952; written widely on Gaelic
literature; published many books especially through Gairm
Publications; four collections of verse, collected poems, *Creachadh
na Clàrsaich*. Hopes to publish new collection shortly.

I have written a good deal about politics and religion, as well as love
of individuals and love of place, and would have liked to bring my
engagement with the Perthshire mountains, Scottish patriotism, the
ties of language and history and place, and the cut and thrust of
politics into this short selection. But it seemed to me that my best
political poems are too extended for the space available, and that
such a sequence as 'The Ark of the Covenant', which explores
religion as it used to be seen in Lewis, needs the internal contrasts
that a sequence can provide. So I have settled for two love-poems,
one early and in regular metre, another a little later and freer in
form, a poem about Lewis (or rather the impossibility of return to a
certain version of Lewis), and 'The Herring Girls', which voices
both love and admiration, together with a black anger at social and
historical prejudice. I have been drawn both to metrical
craftsmanship of the older kind, and to freer structures which have
their own rules and subtleties, and these poems range over some of
the options in that respect also.

CLANN-NIGHEAN AN SGADAIN

An gàire mar chraiteachan salainn
ga fhroiseadh bho 'm beul,
an sàl 's am picil air an teanga,
's na miaran cruinne, goirid a dhèanadh giullachd,
no a thogadh leanabh gu socair, cuimir,
seasgair, fallain,
gun mhearachd,
's na sùilean cho domhainn ri fèath.

B'e bun-os-cionn na h-eachdraidh a dh'fhàg iad
'nan tràillean aig ciùrairean cutach,
thall 's a-bhos air Galldachd 's an Sasainn.
Bu shaillte an duais a thàrr iad
às na mìltean bharaillean ud,
gaoth na mara geur air an craiceann,
is eallach a' bhochdainn 'nan ciste,
is mura b'e an gàire
shaoileadh tu gu robh an teud briste.

Ach bha craiteachan uaille air an cridhe,
ga chumail fallain,
is bheireadh cutag an teanga
slisinn à fanaid nan Gall –
agus bha obair rompa fhathast
nuair gheibheadh iad dhachaigh,
ged nach biodh maoin ac':
air oidhche robach gheamhraidh,
ma bha siud an dàn dhaibh,
dhèanadh iad daoine.

THE HERRING GIRLS

Their laughter like a sprinkling of salt
showered from their lips,
brine and pickle on their tongues,
and the stubby short fingers that could handle fish,
or lift a child gently, neatly,
safely, wholesomely,
unerringly,
and the eyes that were as deep as a calm.

The topsy-turvy of history had made them
slaves to short-arsed curers,
here and there in the Lowlands, in England.
Salt the reward they won
from those thousands of barrels,
the sea-wind sharp on their skins,
and the burden of poverty in their kists,
and were it not for their laughter
you might think the harp-string was broken.

But there was a sprinkling of pride on their hearts,
keeping them sound,
and their tongues' gutting knife
would tear a strip from the Lowlanders' mockery –
and there was work awaiting them
when they got home,
though they had no wealth:
on a wild winter's night,
if that were their lot,
they would make men.

EADAR SAMRADH IS FOGHAR

Os cionn na mara, an lagan uaigneach,
tha glasach far an deach feur a dhochann
air latha samhraidh nach fhalbh às m'inntinn,
ach nuair nì mi cnuasachd air feur 's air fochann
chan fhan am foghar dhomh anns na cruachan,
's cha till an samhradh a dh'aindeoin m'innleachd.

Bha am muir fodham, gach geal 's gach dearg dhith,
gach sumainn tonn-gheal 's gach claisean dùbhghorm,
teicheadh is dlùthadh,
aoibhneas is anail air mhùchadh,
ag at 's a' briseadh,
is slàinte 'na chiùrradh;
is ghlac mi tiota
gu smuain thoirt air a' chaochlaidheachd
bha sìnte fodham,
is air an t-seasmhachd
a chì mi 'n diugh a bha mi uile dh' easbhaidh.

Mi smuaineachadh air dath na grèine,
is dath an fheòir,
is dath na fala a bh' air do bhilean,
is dath an dòchais a bha mi sireadh,
is dath an adhair os cionn Ile,
is dath na sìorraidheachd 's i 'n sin 'na sìneadh.

BETWEEN SUMMER AND AUTUMN

Up from the sea, in a lonely hollow,
is a patch of grass where the shoots were bruised
on a summer's day I can never forget;
but when I garner both grass and corn,
autumn does stay for me in the stacks,
nor will summer return though I will it so.

The sea lay below me, white and red,
white-skinned wave-crest and dark-blue trough,
withdrawing and nearing,
joy with its breath held,
swelling and breaking,
with healing in its hurting;
and I grasped a moment
to think of the mutability
that lay below me,
and to think of the constancy
that I see now I utterly lacked.

I am thinking now of the colour of the sun,
and the colour of the grass,
and the blood-red colour of your lips,
and the colour of the hope that I was seeking,
and the colour of the sky above Islay,
and the colour of eternity lying there.

NUAIR A THILLEAS MI

Nuair a thilleas mi
bidh 'm bàrr-gùg air a' bhuntàt',
bidh 'n t-seillean a' crònan,
bidh 'bhò a' muathal gu eadradh
nuair a thilleas mi.

Nuair a ruigeas mi,
a' breith air làimh oirbh,
bidh fuachd na fàinne
air deàrn an dòchais
nuair a ruigeas mi.

Nuair a laigheas mi
an com do charthannais,
thig an gug-gùg
's an o-draochan maille ris
an uair a laigheas mi.

'S an uair a dh'èireas mi
air a' mhadainn ud,
bidh 'n fhàinne sgealbt'
is a' bhò gun bhainn' aice,
's an t-eilean riabhach mar bu chiad aithne dhomh.

WHEN I COME BACK

When I come back
the potato flowers will be out,
the bees humming,
the cows lowing to milking
when I come back.

When I arrive,
shaking you by the hand,
the coldness of the ring
will be on the palm of hope
when I arrive.

When I lie down
in your kind breast,
the cuckoo will come
and wailing with it,
when I lie down.

And when I rise
on that morning,
the ring will be shattered
and the cow dry,
and the dark-brown island as I first knew it.

MIDGE URE

'I was fourteen when I decided I wanted to do something with my life,' says Midge Ure. At fifteen he left school and started training as an engineer. At eighteen he joined a full-time rock band. He has never looked back since. He has played in a number of bands including Slik, The Rich Kids, Visage and the vastly successful Ultravox. The video for 'Vienna' was a landmark in the pop video industry and gave him the opportunity to direct videos for numerous artists, such as The Funboy Three, Bananarama and Phil Lynott. He co-wrote the 'Do They Know It's Christmas?' single with Bob Geldof. As a trustee of the Band Aid Trust, he has been closely involved with the famine relief operation in Africa. He made the transition from performer to musical director in 1987 for the Prince's Trust Concert at Wembley. In 1988 he put together a 'supergroup' for the Nelson Mandela Concert at Wembley Stadium. His solo single 'If I Was' went to Number One in the UK charts and became an international hit, and 'The Gift' album reached Number Two in the UK charts.

'All Fall Down' (published by Mood Music Ltd). Recorded with The Chieftains, this single was released in November 1986.

'Remembrance Day' (co-written by Danny Mitchell. Published by Mood Music Ltd/Warner Chappell Music Ltd/SBK Songs Ltd). Midge says, 'It's about the horrors of Enniskillen. Religion seems to cause more trouble than ease suffering. Glasgow is like Belfast. In Glasgow I used to get stopped in the streets by gangs who asked me what football team I supported. If you supported Celtic you were a Catholic. Most of the time I had my guitar case with me so I used to say I'm into music. But if they were looking to give you a punch in the mouth you got it.'

'The Leaving (So Long)' (published by Mood Music Ltd/Warner Chappell Music Ltd). Before becoming a teen star in Slik, Midge Ure studied for two and a half years as an apprentice electrical engineer in Glasgow. Midge says, 'I was led to believe that if I left school and got an apprenticeship I wouldn't have any worries. Now people doing the same thing find they have nothing at the end of it. They are forced to leave home and search for work.'

ALL FALL DOWN

When I was a boy there's a dream that I had
That a war if it's fought was for good against bad
And I woke up to find that the world had gone mad
And we'll all fall down.

And I feel like a child again sitting observing
You're toying with power, your fingers are burning
You're pushing so hard that the worms won't be turning
We'll all fall down.

While you try to pretend you're a god upon high
With your party ideals and your squeaky clean lies
When it comes to the crunch you're no smarter than I
And we'll all fall down.

If it's colour or creed or your old time religion
Well fighting for that shows a pure lack of vision
The fight that we strive is the fight to survive
And we'll all fall down.

Well look in the mirror and what do you see
An American, Russian, a soldier or me
When you've all pressed the buttons just where will you be
When we all fall down.

It gets harder to see just what future's in store for us
Hard to see through all the wool you put over us
Words that you give are just words to console us
We'll all fall down.

And what will you do when you've pulled the release
When the sound of thunder has drowned out the pleas
'Cos after all that was your idea of peace
When we all fall down.

No sun for a world that once stood still
No wind's going to blow and no rain's going to fall
No flowers for graves, in fact no graves at all
When we all fall down.

REMEMBRANCE DAY

While I was standing I saw
Two men before my eyes, I saw
One man all dressed in lies
One man held green and gold
The other man blue, white and red
And they smiled as they held guns to our heads.

While I was standing I saw
Two men before my eyes
Watch as the rain begins to fall
Like tears from heaven on us all
To clean the sins we've made
And wash them away, wash them away.

While I was standing I saw
Two countries go to war, I saw
Faces of children wondering
What their friends were fighting for
A crowd of people stood in silence
On Remembrance Day and I cried
As they blew them all away.

While I was standing I saw
Two men before my eyes
Watch as the rain begins to fall
Like tears from heaven on us all
To clean the sins we've made
And wash them away, wash them away.

While I was standing I saw
Two men with one God to share
Both wanting peace by war
Both want to win by prayer
How long before they find
This holy war a heinous sin
And they find that there's nothing left to win.

THE LEAVING (SO LONG)

I'll walk away from my town
See which way the wind blows my future – Oh
Find what's before me
There must be something better
Must be something more than I've had so far
Something new, something good, something worth being put here for

So long, so long, so long.

Move into the city
Find myself a job with a purpose – Oh
I'll work for a reason
And hope that reject turns to warm self-respect
And I'll start to live
Live the life that I thought would be mine
From the day I was born

So long, so long, so long.

Find myself a partner
Turn my partner into a family – Oh
We'll grow old together
Then I'll know that it can be
All that it should be and then
And only then I'll know that I've had
What by rights is mine

So long, so long, so long.

'All Fall Down' appears on the Ultravox album, *UVOX*, Cat. No. CDL 1545.
'Remembrance Day' and 'The Leaving (So Long)' appear on Midge Ure's album
Answers to Nothing, Cat. No. CHR 1649.

KENNETH WHITE

Born Glasgow, 1936. Raised on West coast of Scotland. Studied
languages, literature and philosophy at the universities of Glasgow,
Munich, Paris. Began publishing in London, 1966. Left Scotland for
France in 1967. Work since then published mainly in France (poetry
always in bilingual editions) and from there translated into various
other European languages.

Médicis Etranger prize for *La Route bleue* (*Blue Road North*, based
on a trip to Labrador) in 1983; Grand Prix du rayonnement français
de l'Académie Française for the totality of his work (poetry,
narrative, essay) in 1985; Prix Alfred de Vigny for *Atlantica*, 1987.
After seventeen years in the Pyrenees, now living on the north coast
of Brittany. Holds Chair of Twentieth Century Poetics at the
Sorbonne.

Contact at present being renewed with British intellectual and
cultural scene. A collected longer poem, *The Bird Path*, along with a
prose book, *Travels in the Drifting Dawn*, will be out from
Mainstream (Edinburgh) in the spring of 1989.

Why these poems? Well, I thought: three pages, so better shorts –
ten to twenty-liners. A little geography of the mind, some elective
affinities. Beginning with Erigena, that clear-minded poet-thinker
who, in the ninth century, left Ireland for France where he became a
leading figure in the Carolingian renaissance. Thereafter, breaking
(mental) walls and walking along coastlines: north, south, east and
west. Landscapes, mindscapes. In fact, these poems are from a
collected short poems, *Handbook for the Diamond Country*, I am
at present getting together.

REPORT TO ERIGENA

'Sunt lumina'

'Labour' suddenly seems exactly right
hard slogging, no facility
like learning the basis of a grammar
working your way into unknown logic

it's earth in labour makes for diamond

here on this nameless shore, knowing the work
who are the workers? who the travellers?
reality works – wonders? travel-travail

the old signs come out of the morning
the skull fills and empties with the tide
energy gathered, the first act

ragged coast, rugged, rough winds
the language bears us, bares us

rock province, roots – and lights.

NEW MOON

These walls have grown sullen, and I
lodged between a dairy and an antique shop
between a station and a library, read
no future, live no present, sick
with a bellyful of memory, my skull
like an old tin can that rattles, yet

the sun will move northwards, rising
in the frozen heavens, and the day
will lengthen. New at the month's
beginning, the moon, on the fifteenth night
being close to earth and very full
will raise the tides like whales along the coast.

INTELLECTUAL GATHERING

I've read much hindu literature
over the past few years
close on a hundred well-studied books
but when I stood there with the girl
in the dark blue sari
and might have been expected
in that intellectual gathering
to make some appropriate conversation
all I could think of
was the dark blue sari
and her nakedness under it.

BREST

1.
Brest
midnight
in the *Dead Man's Bar*

'another shot of that lousy red!'

2.
Suddenly
here I am
in the Glasgow Road

and three mad ghosts
walking by my side.

THE WALLS OF AN OLD ROOM

On the first wall
was a print of Hokusai

on the second
was an X-ray photo of my ribs

on the third
was a long quotation from Nietzsche

on the fourth
was nothing at all –

that's the wall I went through
before I arrived here.

A HIGH BLUE DAY ON SCALPAY

This is the summit of contemplation, and
    no art can touch it
blue, so blue, the far-out archipelago, and
    the sea shimmering, shimmering
no art can touch it, the mind can only
    try to become attuned to it
to become quiet, and space itself out, to
    become open and still, unworlded
knowing itself in the diamond country, in
    the ultimate unlettered light.

ACKNOWLEDGEMENTS

The editor and publisher would like to thank the poets for selecting and giving permission to reproduce their material.

Thanks are also due to Aberdeen University Press, Bloodaxe Books, Canongate Publishing Ltd, Carcanet Press Ltd, Chatto & Windus Ltd, Edinburgh University Press, Editions Grasset, Faber & Faber Ltd, Macdonald Publishers (Edinburgh), Mood Music Ltd, Oxford University Press, Peterloo Poets, Polygon Books, Ramsey Head Press, Secker & Warburg Ltd, and Workshop Press.

Every effort has been made to trace and acknowledge copyright-holders, but if any have inadvertently been overlooked the publisher will be pleased to make the necessary arrangements at the first opportunity.